REMOTE AND HYBRID WORK

WHAT EVERYONE NEEDS TO KNOW®

REMOTE AND HYBRID WORK

WHAT EVERYONE NEEDS TO KNOW®

BARBARA Z. LARSON

OXFORD
UNIVERSITY PRESS

OXFORD
UNIVERSITY PRESS

Oxford University Press is a department of the University of Oxford. It furthers
the University's objective of excellence in research, scholarship, and education
by publishing worldwide. Oxford is a registered trade mark of Oxford University
Press in the UK and certain other countries.

"What Everyone Needs to Know" is a registered trademark of
Oxford University Press.

Published in the United States of America by Oxford University Press
198 Madison Avenue, New York, NY 10016, United States of America.

Library of Congress Control Number: 2023942436
ISBN 978–0–19–768496–2 (pbk.)
ISBN 978–0–19–768495–5 (hbk.)

DOI: 10.1093/wentk/9780197684955.001.0001

Paperback printed by Sheridan Books, Inc., United States of America
Hardback printed by Bridgeport National Bindery, Inc., United States of America

This book is dedicated to my son, Emil,
who makes everything worthwhile.

CONTENTS

INTRODUCTION

My interest in remote work has spanned the majority of my professional career, even though I didn't begin working from home until 2005. My first experience dealing with a version of remote work occurred in the late 1980s, when I worked as an assistant in the trademark licensing arm of Hearst Magazines. My job involved what today we would call virtual communication, in that most of my interactions with licensees took place either by fax or by phone. I often went months or years without meeting licensees in person (and a few I never met), yet I managed to develop strong professional relationships with many of them. At the time, I was struck by the fact that one of my favorite relationships was with a Japanese agent with whom I mainly interacted by fax. Yet, our two in-person meetings over four years created a bond that felt stronger than most others, even those with clients who were geographically closer to our New York City office.

Later, as I moved into international financial management roles, first at FMC Corporation and then at R. R. Donnelley, many of my closest collaborators were geographically dispersed, across countries and time zones. Even though I was not working from home, I conducted most of my business communication through technology, now email and telephone. In the late 1990s, my employer gave me a laptop computer, which suddenly allowed me to work nearly everywhere—for better and for worse.

In the early 2000s, I began to experience the downsides of extensive virtual and remote work. Due in part to travel, and in part to my own impatience and naivete, my relationships with some of my colleagues in my home office at R. R. Donnelley began to fray. I became known among some for sending sharply worded emails, often copying in others for emphasis, even to people who worked just one floor away from me in the same building. Finally, in 2004, my manager gave me the first mediocre performance appraisal I had received in decades. "It's your emails," he noted. "You're great to work with in person, but something happens when you start sending emails."

This feedback caught my attention, but also sparked my curiosity. What was that "something" that was happening? Certainly, part of it was my tendency toward impatience, but something else was causing me to depersonalize my colleagues, making me feel comfortable writing things in emails that I never would have said if we had been meeting in person. Shortly thereafter, I opted to enter academia as a way to reduce my travel while also increasing the variety and challenge of my work. I loved working in international finance, but I wanted to explore other facets of work life, particularly those related to human behavior.

After several years researching other topics, I came back to the issue of virtual and remote work through a teaching question. Shortly after joining Northeastern University's D'Amore-McKim School of Business in 2012, I began to revise an Organizational Behavior teaching plan. I realized that I wanted to teach my students how to work with dispersed others. I assumed that this would be important to their careers, given increases in communication technology and globalization of business. And I wanted them to avoid some of the mistakes that I had made.

Given that management professors tend to produce—and generously share—large amounts of teaching ideas and materials, I was surprised to find almost nothing related to virtual or remote work. I then went to the research to try to put something together myself. Here, I found some of the answers that I had sought in the many studies cited throughout this book. I was particularly inspired by research on the individual experience of virtuality and remoteness, including work by Jeanne Wilson and Tim Golden, among many others. I also found a community of scholars who were just as fascinated by, and curious about, the phenomena of remoteness and virtuality as I was.

In 2013, I met my longtime research collaborator and co-author, Erin Makarius, at a teaching conference where we were each leading workshops related to teaching virtual and remote work skills. I have been lucky to work with Erin on a number of projects, both academic and practice-oriented, as well as other leading researchers in the field, such as Raj Choudhury, Travis Maynard, Lucy Gilson, and Sharon Hill.

In the spring of 2020, our relatively niche research community was rocked by the sudden shift of more than half a billion workers around the world to remote work due to the onset of the COVID-19 pandemic. As intense and exciting as it was to experience the sudden interest in the principles and practices of our field of research, it was even more exciting to see remote work—and its new cousin, hybrid work—becoming institutionalized in many sectors of the economy, even as pandemic restrictions lifted. The rise of remote work since 2020 may be viewed by future historians as one of the largest-scale disruptions in work life since the advent of the personal computer. Unquestionably, it has changed the lives and the work experiences of millions of people around the world.

Today, whether you work remotely or not, it is likely that virtual and remote work affects your professional life. You may be located in a different office location from your manager or colleagues, communicating largely by email, chat, and videoconference. Your co-workers may spend part or all their time working from home. Your clients may no longer wish to meet for business lunches, opting instead for Zoom calls. Your business travel, essentially eliminated during the early years of the pandemic, has likely not returned to its pre-pandemic levels, while invitations to virtual meetings, conferences, and webinars have ballooned. If you work in technology or at a professional services firm, you may now even be attending training or meetings in a virtual metaverse setting.

This book was written to provide a wide-ranging foundational view of the past, present, and future of remote and hybrid work for working professionals, students, and interested observers alike. It is my hope that with this overview of remote and hybrid work you may appreciate—and participate in—this aspect of our work world in a more satisfying way.

The number of people who directly or indirectly contributed to this book is vast; I will name just a few here but am grateful to all.

I could not have asked for a better editor than Daniel Luzer at Oxford University Press, who first approached me with the book idea, and then shepherded me with encouragement and expert advice through the entire writing process. His guidance and editing improved the manuscript, and his support was so appreciated by this first-time author.

I was lucky to have wonderful research assistance while working on this book, including the indomitable Stella

Klingebiel, Cassidy Webb, and Maria Zapata Perez. I also thank Raj Choudhury, Ioannis Ioannou, Prashanth Saka, and Leslie Shannon for advice on particular aspects of the manuscript. Any errors, however, are mine alone.

A sabbatical grant from Northeastern University gave me time to write a large part of the book, and an unrestricted gift from Clean Harbors, Inc. has allowed me to explore new aspects of remote work in recent years; for all this support, I am grateful. I am honored to have such supportive and intellectually challenging colleagues in the Management and Organizational Development group at the D'Amore-McKim School of Business. I am similarly thankful every day to work with the driven and brilliant students that I am lucky enough to teach there.

As a relative latecomer to academia, I have truly appreciated the mentorship of Professors Amy Edmondson, Cynthia Lee, Ed Wertheim, Jamie Ladge, Jordan Siegel, among others. My research collaboration with Erin Makarius over the past decade has expanded my knowledge and greatly increased my enjoyment of what is sometimes solitary work.

I owe a great debt to the business leaders who (through both words and actions) taught me so much about virtual and remote work during my years in industry. Jack Heistand, Eric Evans, Stephanie Kushner, and Joseph Lawler, among others, invested their time in my professional development and gave me opportunities to work in international settings with far-flung colleagues and clients. I am particularly grateful to Greg Stoklosa, then CFO of R. R. Donnelley, whose much-needed developmental feedback about my virtual communication style sparked my initial interest in researching virtual and remote work.

This book would not have been possible without the care and encouragement of my family and friends. My mother and father, Rebecca Zepp and the late Glenn Zepp, instilled in me a passion for books and learning—anything that I do well in my academic career started with them. I also thank Martha, Dave Z, Sabine, Laura, David T, Ilene, Prash, Sara, Tina, and Reem for always knowing the right thing to say, and for taking my calls even when I haven't returned theirs for weeks. My son, Emil, in his teenage wisdom, helps me retain perspective on what matters most. My partner, Arthur Gaer, has been unfailingly supportive through months of writing weekends, always knowing when to bring me caffeine and when to crack a sly joke to keep me going. I thank him from the bottom of my heart.

1

INTRODUCTION TO REMOTE
AND HYBRID WORK

What is remote work?

Remote work is the work people do when separated geographically from co-workers. The most familiar form of remote work in the twenty-first century is working from home. However, remote work doesn't always mean working from your actual living space; it can mean any kind of work arrangement in which someone is in a different location than other members of their organization.

People call remote work lots of different things, including telecommuting, telework, distributed work, e-work, and, in some countries, Smart Working. While there are distinctions between these terms, in practice people use them almost interchangeably. This book will use the term "remote work" to encompass all these terms, with the defining characteristic of physical separation from the employer.

When did remote work begin, and what changed because of the COVID-19 pandemic?

Working from home was the dominant model of labor long before the advent of offices. Throughout much of human history, people have worked and lived in the same place, as farmers, hunters, artisans, or in other independent occupations. Earlier peoples focused on subsistence (self-sustaining activities), while in later centuries home-based workers traded goods with each other.

Researchers have documented a few office-type structures in Ancient Rome and many more during the Renaissance period in Europe. But it was the first Industrial Revolution in the mid-nineteenth century that established the office as a primary location for work. The second Industrial Revolution, in the early twentieth century, brought huge numbers of workers into large offices. This work model prevailed through the 1970s.

Jack Nilles, a research director at the University of Southern California, began the first experiments with remote working in the mid-1970s.[1] Nilles is often credited as the creator of the term "telecommuting." His research emerged from concern about the impact of long commute times on both workers and the environment.[2] Nilles and his research team experimented with a national insurance company. The results suggested that telecommuting could increase productivity and retention of employees, while reducing air pollution and energy consumption.[3] But there was no home computing technology back then. Indeed, Nilles first conceptualized telecommuting as companies sending employees to locations close to their houses, in small groups, instead of working from central offices.[4]

IBM, which did have access to cutting-edge computing technology, was responsible for the next major development in remote work. In 1979 the company allowed five employees from its Santa Teresa Laboratory facility in Silicon Valley to work at home with company-provided computer terminals. IBM developed this pilot project because of concerns about its retention of engineers and programmers. The company developed a similar pilot on the East Coast because of computing capacity limits in its offices.[5]

By 1983, some two thousand IBM employees worked remotely.[6] Around the same time, retailer JCP enney allowed
its telephone-based customer service agents to begin
working from home.[7]

In subsequent decades companies became more comfortable with remote work as mainframe-linked computer
terminals gave way to personal computing and then to
portable computers and laptops. The share of full days
worked from home by the US workforce nearly tripled
from 1980 to 2000, but remained relatively small, estimated
at 1.7 percent of all workdays, in 2000.[8]

By the early 2000s, further advances in voice and video
communications increased remote workers' ability to collaborate with others. The start of Skype in 2003 greatly
democratized the availability of voice-over-internet-
protocol (VOIP) audio and video calling, allowing people
to hold meetings for little or no cost, even if they or their
employers did not own expensive videoconferencing
equipment. WebEx (later owned by Cisco and rebranded
"Webex"), which had up to then focused primarily on the
high-value large-corporate market, broadened its customer
base by acquiring a smaller competitor with an existing
customer base of small and medium-sized businesses.
They also added elements, such as document-sharing and
instant messaging, to create what one news outlet called
"the 'Cadillac' of web conferencing services."[9]

Even as technological advances plateaued in the
2010s, the prevalence of remote work continued to grow,
increasing from 1.7 percent in 2000 to approximately
2.8 percent of full workdays in the United States in 2010.
But many employees found the structures and rules of
remote work frustrating. Many companies allowed such
work on an ad-hoc basis, with few or no organizational
policies. The inconsistencies that resulted (companies
gave some departments or individuals more flexibility

than others) led both employees and managers to express concerns about fairness. In a 2010 interview with a tech industry newsletter, one manager lamented that not all employees "have the desire to excel. If I provide telecommunicating privileges to the one who does, then I have to do the same for that employee who is not as dedicated. We are forced to be 'fair' and treat all employees the same."[10] Managers and executives began to complain of deterioration in both employee productivity and collaboration.[11]

On February 22, 2013, Kara Swisher, writing for the *Wall Street Journal*'s "All Things D" technology blog, reported that the online media company Yahoo! (then led by CEO Marissa Mayer) was going to require its remote employees to return to the office beginning in June of that year.[12] Later that day came a memo from the firm's head of human resources, Jackie Reses.[13] The memo read in part:

> To become the absolute best place to work, communication and collaboration will be important, so we need to be working side-by-side. That is why it is critical that we are all present in our offices. Some of the best decisions and insights come from hallway and cafeteria discussions, meeting new people, and impromptu team meetings. Speed and quality are often sacrificed when we work from home. We need to be one Yahoo!, and that starts with physically being together.

Most media coverage criticized the move, directing particular vitriol at Mayer. "Back to the Stone Age?" asked a *Forbes* headline, and *The Guardian*'s Emma Keller called the memo "offensive," and the new policy "clunky and out-of-date."[14]

Despite the initial backlash, for several years following Yahoo!'s move, other large employers announced transitions away from remote work. Best Buy eliminated its "Results-Only Work Environment" remote work program just eleven days after Yahoo!'s announcement. In 2014 the online forum company Reddit required its remote working employees to relocate to San Francisco or be terminated.[15] Insurance giant Aetna, which in 2013 had gone on record as a staunch supporter of remote work, reversed its position in 2016.[16] Even IBM, arguably the pioneer of corporate telecommuting, announced a significant reduction in the number of its remote jobs in 2017.[17]

Companies that explained their retreats from remote work typically focused on concerns about reduced productivity and a lack of creativity and collaboration. However, some business writers observed that the companies reducing remote work privileges were also typically experiencing significant business downturns or other existential threats, and they speculated that the policy changes were perhaps a misguided attempt to return the firms to their old glory. Such policies could also have been a way to induce some employees to quit their jobs, reducing the need for costly layoffs.[18]

Even as media coverage of remote work gave the appearance of a retreat in the mid-2010s, the overall prevalence of the practice continued to rise during this time. In 2019, people worked remotely just under 5 percent of all full workdays.[19]

After years of slow but steady increases in remote work, the COVID-19 pandemic brought a transformational change within a matter of weeks. With most of the developed world shutting down in-person gatherings in March 2020, remote work emerged as the only viable option for many. At the height of the initial pandemic lockdown period, in April 2020, approximately 62 percent of

US employees worked from home full-time, representing a twelvefold increase from the pre-pandemic estimate. As COVID-19 mitigation strategies became more common, the prevalence of remote work in the United States decreased, leveling off as of late 2022 at around 29 percent.[20]

Remote work is common in other industrialized countries, while economic and cultural differences lead to considerable variation across nations. One survey conducted in early 2022 suggests that the United States was at about the midpoint of days per week worked remotely. Korea, Taiwan, Egypt, and Serbia reported considerably lower levels. Remote work is much more common in Canada, India, and Singapore.[21]

What did employers learn about remote work from the COVID-19 pandemic?

While different companies responded to the pandemic very differently (it makes much more sense to let employees work remotely if you run a technology startup, for example, than if you administer a hospital), there were a few common lessons for employers.

First, people realized quickly (sometimes to their surprise) how much work people could do remotely. A *New York Times Magazine* article from June 2020 profiled Josh Harcus, a robotic vacuum cleaner salesman who adapted quickly to the lockdown environment by creating a virtual demo of his product, via "a looping image of the robot zipping around a hotel, which he ran in Zoom's 'virtual background,' while his face and torso floated in front of it." To his (and his employer SoftBank Robotics') delight, sales remained strong.[22]

Second, managers and executives who had never worked remotely received a crash course in both managing remote employees and in being remote workers themselves. In some cases, this experience caused leaders to recognize the potential benefits of remote work as a longer-term labor strategy, leading to new post-pandemic policies allowing more flexibility in work location. Mark Benioff, CEO of software provider Salesforce, noted in a mid-2021 interview that "the companies and our customers are successful. It's incredible, but the way they're being successful has completely changed." Benioff suggested that few employees were returning to offices because they could do their jobs just as well from home. Salesforce earnings were higher than expected during the same period and the company's stock price rose accordingly.[23]

In other cases, however, executives expressed considerable frustration with their own experience with remote work, which often appeared to reinforce existing biases against it. A notorious example of this frustration were comments from David Solomon, CEO of the investment banking firm Goldman Sachs. Solomon complained that a junior banker at his firm had approached and introduced himself to Solomon in the summer of 2020 during a weekday lunch at a restaurant in the Hamptons.[24] There were no apparent threats to business performance, as Goldman's share price was rising along with much of the market at that time,[25] and Solomon himself was dining in the same restaurant at the same time. Yet, the CEO cited this story numerous times as evidence for the failure of remote work as a labor model; because Goldman Sachs employees were spending their workdays dining out in a resort town, they were in his view taking advantage of COVID-19 protocols and not working hard enough.

Finally, the COVID-19 pandemic made job, and often class, distinctions very clear. First responders, healthcare professionals, and laborers in the manufacture of essential goods risked—and lost—their lives daily in the early months of the pandemic. Many restaurant and hospitality workers lost their jobs altogether. But even as newly remote workers struggled with the challenges of new technology, social isolation, or parenting while working, they were still better off because they had the privilege of a job that allowed for remote work. This work disparity probably contributed to the wave of resignations and job changes during 2020–2022, often referred to as the "Great Resignation."[26] A 2021 survey conducted by The Conference Board, a US-based think tank, found that 24 percent of participants who had quit jobs during the pandemic had done so because they wanted to work remotely.[27]

Why can some pandemic-era research on remote work be less helpful?

As we move on in upcoming chapters to a review of the factors influencing remote work, and remote work's effects on individuals, work products, and organizations, you might notice there's relatively little discussion of pandemic-era remote work. This omission is intentional because much research from that era has limitations for explaining remote work in general.

During the lockdown periods of 2020 and early 2021, many people tried to balance work at home with childcare because schools moved to remote learning and daycares closed. In the earliest days of the pandemic, many local governments and local providers suspended services typically available to support working professionals (such as housecleaning, babysitting, and even food delivery). As a result, it is probably not surprising that researchers found increased stress levels, higher work levels, and greater work–family conflict during this time period. These findings are certainly important as a historical snapshot of an extraordinary period. They are less helpful for understanding the experience of normal remote work during times when children are at school and normal support structures are in place.

An important part of evaluating research is to question how findings can be generalized, and how well they apply in situations different from the research setting. In this case, research about work habits, attitudes, coping mechanisms, and job performance during the COVID-19 era is better generalized to other situations involving adaptation during a crisis, rather than situations involving people working remotely. If I mention pandemic-era research in future chapters, it's because it contains insights that survive these limitations.

What types of remote work arrangements exist?

One of the challenges in both researching and tracking remote work practices is that remote work arrangements take different forms. Below are some common remote work arrangements.

Working from home is the most commonly known form of remote work. A person engaging in such work operates from their living space or a location near it, rather than from a traditional office, for some or all of their normal working hours. Before the pandemic, the Bureau of Labor Statistics estimated that 4 to 5 percent of the US working population had some type of formal work-from-home arrangement.[28] As of mid-2022, this estimate was closer to 30 percent of the population, after spiking to more than 60 percent during the height of COVID-19 lockdowns in 2020.[29]

Despite its name, work from home doesn't always occur at home; it can also involve an employee working at a third location like a coffee shop or a co-working space. While coffee shops have long been a favorite location for remote workers, the increased prevalence and extent of remote work post-pandemic led firms to explore alternative work sites near employees' homes. In early 2022, the co-working space provider WeWork projected a 30 percent increase in its annual revenue due to increased demand from companies looking to provide flexible work locations to employees.[30]

At least in the context of remote and hybrid work, work from home does not include the occasional evening or weekend time spent working at home (to supplement a full workweek in the office). This distinction has not always been made clear in statistical reporting of home-based working, leading to inflated estimates of remote work in the United States. Until recently, the US government's Bureau of Labor Statistics' primary question related to remote work asked participants to report simply whether they had performed any of their work at home on the day of the survey.[31] Thus, a teacher who brought home papers to grade after dinner would be counted as equivalent to someone who worked remotely every day.

Hybrid work refers to a condition of part-remote, part-in-office work—in essence, it is part-time remote work. The term "hybrid work" and "hybrid workplace" became popularized during the later stages of the COVID-19 pandemic, as many people started to return to the office. In the United States, as of late 2022, the average hybrid worker spent 2.8 days per week working from home.[32]

Work from anywhere is a work arrangement in which employees are not required to live near their employer's location and instead can work remotely from a location of their choosing. Generally, such arrangements require employees to live within the same country or even region.[33] For example, the US government, a pioneer in experimenting with work-from-anywhere jobs, requires employees to be located in the continental United States. Some companies, such as Airbnb and Wikimedia

Foundation, have gone further and allowed employees to live anywhere they want in the world.[34] Work-from-anywhere arrangements have become more common in recent years, particularly in the technology industry, but the prevalence of such arrangements is still low enough that statistics are not available. However, current numbers will likely increase. The work-from-anywhere trajectory appears similar to that of work-from-home, with low numbers in the first years and rapid growth as workers and employers discover how well it can work.

What is "virtual communication" and "virtuality" and how is this different from remote work?

Among discussions and media coverage of remote work, you may occasionally hear references to its close cousin, virtual work or virtual communication. Virtual communication refers to the use of technology to share ideas and information with others. Our ability to communicate using technology is what allows us to work remotely.

But the term "technology" simply means the use of knowledge to invent things or solve problems. With that in mind, virtual communication has been around since long before email and videoconferencing. In eighteenth- and nineteenth-century commerce, workers used early forms of technology to communicate with each other and with customers and suppliers through much slower means, such as handwritten letters sent by messenger (locally), carrier pigeons (regionally), and transoceanic shipping (globally). Historians still debate the impact of early technologies on the development of global business.[35]

Virtual work is much more widespread in today's workplace than people commonly realize. People who use email or even telephone calls for their jobs, as almost everyone does, are engaging in virtual work. Whether or not someone is in the office full-time, they will experience the challenge and effects of virtual work just as much as people who work from their kitchen tables every day or have never been to a main office to meet with colleagues.

Sometimes the terms "virtual work" and "remote work" are used interchangeably, but it should now be obvious that remote work is just one subset of virtual work. When we discuss remoteness and remote work in future chapters, we will focus on the physical separation from co-workers. When we discuss virtual communication and virtuality, we will focus on the use of technology to communicate, which is relevant to remote workers and most in-office workers alike.

2

THE INDIVIDUAL'S EXPERIENCE OF VIRTUALITY AND VIRTUAL COMMUNICATION

This chapter focuses on virtual communication—interactions that take place using technology, *regardless of location*. Even if you are located just steps away from your co-workers, you may find yourself communicating with them virtually, whether to save time, to include others in the conversation, or to retain a record of what was said.

In Chapter 1 we noted that nearly everyone engages in some sort of virtual communication, ranging from phone calls and emails to sophisticated video conferencing or even immersive-reality meetings. Nearly everyone also notices differences between virtual and in-person communication, and many people struggle with those differences.

How is communicating virtually with someone different from face-to-face interaction?

Think about the types of virtual communication that you have experienced yourself, whether texting, email chains, phone conversations, or videoconferencing via a platform such as Zoom or Webex. How was it different from communicating with someone face-to-face?

When asked this question, most people immediately note that they have less information about their conversation partner in virtual communication. Sometimes people also describe a lower-quality relationship related to several different factors. They may find it difficult to figure out when and how to communicate with the other person. They may describe difficulty in trusting someone they haven't met in person and sometimes haven't seen at all. Or, they may say that they just don't have the same type of informal chatting with their virtual counterpart that they do with someone in a face-to-face setting and, as a result, don't enjoy interacting with them as much.

How does virtuality affect interpersonal interactions?

Research on the effects of virtuality in communication began largely in the 1980s, as personal computing and internet use began to take hold. Early researchers noticed that people communicating at work via email or electronic message boards exhibited a striking reduction in normal social inhibitions, leading to behavior that was not typical of their normal in-office work. The research subjects engaged in "flaming" (expressing strong, inflammatory opinions, sometimes accompanied by profanity) and were more comfortable delivering bad news or negative information than they were in person.[1]

More recent research suggests that intensely negative, flaming communications among people who know each other at work have become less common (perhaps we have become more practiced at communicating virtually since the 1980s!)[2] And yet, most of us have at some time experienced the escalation in tension and conflict that can occur in even simple email discussions at work. Indeed, my own interest in studying virtual work stemmed from watching sometimes routine email chains escalating into conflict over years of working in multinational corporations . . . and realizing that I sometimes had been the instigator of the escalation.

Email chains frequently spiral out of control when one person starts expanding the reach of the communication by adding to the distribution list (often by cc'ing the additional recipients). Copying in people who are directly related to the issue at hand is appropriate and often appreciated. These types of additions are typically mentioned in the text of the email itself, along with the reason for inclusion (e.g., "I'm copying Khalid on this, as he is better suited to advise on state regulations").

However, if a sender expands the list of recipients without explaining the reasoning in the email, the action can be interpreted as a tactic of escalation, especially if the people newly brought into the email are of higher status in the organization. If I suddenly copy in my manager, or worse yet, the manager of the person with whom I'm emailing, and I don't explain this new inclusion, my counterparty is very likely to interpret the action as signaling my displeasure or distrust in a passive-aggressive way, akin to gathering the troops in preparation for battle. The next logical move is for my counterparty to do the same, while they also start to think about how to reciprocate their own (perhaps newfound) displeasure and distrust.

In addition to heightening hostility, adding tangential members to an email list decreases productivity for the organization because it requires many more people to not only read the email, but to also try to discern what action is needed. The social and productivity implications of this practice are great enough that the US National Institute of Health's Ombudsman's office opted to cover the topic in its first-ever blog post in August 2020.[3]

In a work setting, digital virtual communication can be particularly perilous because it is so easy for people to share it with others. In March 2022, an executive representing a franchisee of multiple Applebee's restaurants was quickly fired after wide distribution of an email in which he had opined that inflation might make people more willing to work at their restaurants for less money and more hours. The email was forwarded to a restaurant employee initially, who then distributed it to other locations owned by the same franchisee. Within days, both managers and employees had quit their jobs at several locations, and the email was posted on Reddit and Twitter. After Applebee's fired the executive, a spokesperson for the franchisee expressed frustration with the apparent lack of forethought in the original email, saying, "Maybe he wrote it in the middle of the night. I don't know."[4]

It is easy to find more extreme versions of virtual conflict in almost any comment section of a news publication or other public online forum, where virtual conversations can quickly escalate from minor disagreement of opinion to intense, often ad hominem, attacks. Some media organizations, including NPR and *The Atlantic*, have eliminated comment sections because of this tendency.[5] Even seemingly innocuous online discussion sites can be taken over by vicious arguments. The *New York Times'* Cooking Community Facebook group went from being described as the "happy corner of the internet" in 2019 to being abandoned by the publication in 2021, largely due to political and other conflicts that emerged among different factions of its virtual participants.[6]

On the rare occasions when targets confront their online abusers, the abusers frequently turn apologetic and sometimes remorseful. American writer and comedian Lindy West had the opportunity to speak with one of her most persistent online abusers on the NPR show *This American Life*. She later wrote: "He was shockingly self-aware. He told me that . . . he hated me because, to put it simply, I don't hate myself. . . . He said that, at the time [of the trolling], he felt fat, unloved, 'passionless' and purpose-less."[7] Research on cyberbullying finds that aggressive on-line bullies are often people who feel lonely, bored, or have themselves been the victims of bullying.[8]

Why can virtual interactions be so difficult and turn negative so quickly?

Two factors—anonymity and certain cognitive biases—are keys to understanding the deterioration of virtual commu-nication. Virtual interactions are most likely to sour quickly when participants are anonymous, allowing them to es-cape accountability and the consequences of their words.

Virtual anonymity is not common in the workplace, but there have been poor outcomes when it does occur. A dramatic example occurred at Google when engineer Liz Fong-Jones, a longtime critic of Google's inclusion and di-versity policies, announced her resignation from the com-pany. In the weeks between her resignation and departure, a private Google-employee channel in the anonymous dis-cussion app Blind exploded with posts that ranged from criticism of Fong-Jones to anti-Asian jokes and transphobic commentary.[9]

Other companies have reported similar experiences with anonymous performance feedback systems, such as Amazon's "Anytime Feedback Tool."[10] While Amazon's tool is not strictly anonymous, the identity of those submitting negative feedback is typically kept from the employee receiving the feedback, allowing for "a river of intrigue and scheming" without consequences, according to a 2015 *New York Times* article about the company.

Certain cognitive biases also contribute to a greater like-lihood of negative experiences in virtual (versus face-to-face) interactions. Cognitive biases are patterns of error that humans make when interpreting information. These biases can lead to questionable decision-making, including poor word choices and bad behavior. Cognitive biases often occur when people are making decisions based on limited information or when they are pressed for time and need to act quickly. Clearly, both conditions often apply to virtual communications.

One of the most common cognitive biases is "fundamental attribution error." This is the human tendency to explain another person's behavior (undesirable behavior in particular) as a function of their fundamental character, rather than due to external circumstances, more often than is accurate.

For example, if you are driving on the highway, and someone cuts in front of you and causes you to slam on your brakes, what do you immediately think about that person? Most of us would immediately think something about that driver's intelligence, driving skills, or other fundamental character traits. Few people will consider the possibility that an external factor (like poor directions or a personal emergency) had compromised this driver's behavior, and even fewer will assume that there was a valid external circumstance causing the poor driving. Of course, some people are indeed fundamentally bad drivers. Yet it is very unlikely that these people account for every instance of poor driving. Rather, fundamental attribution error leads people to make many more assumptions of poor character in other drivers than are accurate.

People are vulnerable to fundamental attribution error to some degree all the time. But virtuality tends to enhance the risk of this bias, particularly if someone doesn't know their virtual counterpart personally. One school of thought on virtual communication suggests that the extent to which we feel distant from a virtual other might influence our vulnerability to fundamental attribution error and other cognitive biases. The theory that lays out this logic is called construal-level theory.

What is construal-level theory and how does it help explain the challenges of virtual communication?

Construal-level theory comes from psychology and asserts that someone's mental image—or "construal"—of another person is influenced by the extent to which the individual perceives psychological distance between themselves and the other person.[11] When someone else feels psychologically distant, we are likely to perceive them using a "high-level" construal, characterized by abstraction, little detail, and importantly, categorizing the person with others. Conversely, if the other person feels psychologically close, we are more likely to make a lower-level construal, characterized by a high level of individual-specific detail.

Think about someone you feel particularly close to—a close friend, perhaps. Think about how you would describe the image that you have in your mind of this person—most likely, you could give a very detailed description, including things like physical appearance, tone of voice, facial expressions, and behavioral patterns.

Now, think about the last customer service agent you spoke with on the phone. What kind of image can you build in your mind of that person? Most likely, your mind constructs a partial image of a person, perhaps a general body silhouette with no specific facial features, or a generic type of person that you imagine based on the limited information you gained from the call (such as the customer service agent's accent).

What are the differences between these two images? The more accurate image is the lower-level construal you have of the person to whom you feel (and are) more psychologically close. But more important, it is likely that you have slotted the customer service agent into a pre-existing category in your mind, whether based on the agent's apparent regional background, gender, age, or perceived personality traits. You may also have a somewhat depersonalized image of the individual—when I run this exercise with my students, they often mention that they imagine a body form with blurred-out facial features.

How does this help us understand virtual interactions? Research suggests that high-level construals are more likely to result in the cognitive bias of fundamental attribution error and stereotyping in our perceptions of others.[12] When we have a high-level construal of someone, we're more likely to attribute their behavior or opinions to their personal character ("she's an unfriendly person"), rather than to external circumstances ("she must be having a frustrating day").

How does virtuality limit the sharing of information and why does this matter?

In any given interaction, we typically share several types of information, whether we're thinking about it or not. The most obvious of these is information related to the purpose of the communication—let's call that "task-related" information. For example, if you call a co-worker to ask for some historical financial data, that request for data (including the details of the data that you need, the format in which you need it, and the time by which you need it) comprises the task-related information sharing.

It is easy to think of task-related information as the only information shared during an interaction. However, research has shown that another type of information sharing is also important for ensuring high-quality communications—situational information. Situational information describes the conditions—and any challenges—of someone's current working environment. These conditions can include technology features, logistical challenges, competing priorities, supervisor or co-worker pressure, or local events or emergencies, among other factors.[13]

Using the previous example, when you call your co-worker to ask for historical financial data, your situational information might include the fact that your computer has been acting up lately, making it difficult for you to get your work done, and your manager has been checking in on you every hour or two. Your co-worker's situation might include the fact that their elderly parent is in the hospital, and their department is undergoing renovation. Think for a minute about how each of you might feel if these situations existed—and how those emotions might influence your words or behavior.

Here's where virtuality makes things more difficult. In the hypothetical situation above, it turns out that if you both are in the same office, and you drop by your co-worker's desk to make a task-related information request, each of you is more likely to learn parts or all of the other's situational information than you would in a virtual setting. In some cases, the information may be immediately apparent (for instance, distracting construction going on near your co-worker's desk). In other cases, we will observe clues that can lead us to assess the situation fairly quickly (for instance, your co-worker may be obviously distressed when you arrive at their desk or may even be on the phone with the hospital). And just your physical proximity increases the odds that you and your co-worker will engage in some social (non-task-related) interaction, which will likely include situational information.

Now, think about how much of this information might not be apparent in a virtual setting. It is likely you would not share any of this information in an email unless you and your co-worker already know and feel close to each other. On video, some of this information might become apparent, but it is less likely to be observable and can be hidden easily.

Overall, we can generally assess situational information better when we are in person than when we are communicating virtually. But why does this matter? One experimental study involved a simple virtual task that required information sharing among two participants to complete a task. Organizational psychologist Catherine Cramton and her colleagues found in this study that when virtuality limited situational information, people tended to assume that the other person's situation was the *same as their own situation*, even when it wasn't, and just as with high-level construal, people were *more likely to commit fundamental attribution error*, attributing perceived failures or shortfalls to their virtual counterparty's abilities or character, rather than to situational factors.[14]

As part of the design of this experiment, one member of each pair of participants was missing some critical task-related information, unbeknownst to their partner. When the pair were working virtually, and the partner responded slowly or inaccurately due to the missing information, the other person (who had requested the information) was more likely to explain the delay by describing their partner as slow or confused. When participants were physically in the same location, those requesting the information quickly observed and explained (correctly) that their partner did not have access to the needed information; that is, the underperformance was due to the situation.

What can be done to reduce the risk of fundamental attribution error in virtual communication?

The strongest antidote to fundamental attribution error is generally information about the other person involved in an interaction. Investing in even minimal face-to-face interaction can greatly enhance the quality of virtual relationships. In general, face-to-face interaction prevents people from depersonalizing and making negative attributions about each other during later virtual communication (especially communication that is only text-based). In the workplace, face-to-face interaction can also result in a higher level of informal networking, social interaction, and cohesion-building among co-workers.[15]

When an in-person meet-up is not possible, co-workers can also lower construal levels simply by shifting to a communication medium that conveys more information (also known as increasing the "richness" of the medium). A frustrating email chain can often be resolved quickly with an audio conversation or a video call. A disembodied conference call with no video (one consulting client described this to me as a "sea of black squares") can be made more interactive and generate more social cohesion simply by ensuring everyone turns on their video. Moving to a richer medium causes people to share more information, including situational information. This reduces the likelihood of fundamental attribution error.

Finally, people working together virtually often find that they can increase the quality of their relationship and work dramatically by simply sharing some situational information. This sharing does not need to be extensive or detailed, and requests for situational information should not be intrusive. A simple example is to start a call with a fairly generic line like, "How are things going in your neck of the woods today?" to offer the other person an opportunity to share their situation.

You can share situational information in ways that are professional but also helpful. This could be as simple as starting a call with a line such as "I apologize for the noise—there is a major construction project going on next to my office" or "I'm glad we got to speak today, as I've got two different projects due in by tomorrow and am a bit rushed."

While awareness alone is not a cure for cognitive biases, it can be a powerful first step. But we do not yet know whether training workers to recognize the heightened risk of fundamental attribution error—and the steps they can take to mitigate the risk—will have a significant impact on their future virtual communications. Given the continued virtualization of the workplace, it is likely that we will learn more about the effects of training over the next few years.

Are there any advantages of virtual communication?

The biggest obvious advantage of today's digitized virtual communication is that it allows people to transmit information quickly and inexpensively to many different locations. The ability to digitize and transmit video, audio, text, and graphical information between people in different locations has indescribable benefits. It has enabled tremendous advances in communication and collaboration in business, government, and civil society. In most cases, the challenges we have discussed in this chapter are more than offset by the benefits of these capabilities.

Research suggests additional advantages of virtual communication. First, people working together virtually tend to perceive fewer status differences than they do when meeting face-to-face.[16] For example, senior leaders of an organization feel less intimidating to junior employees when they are on a video call rather than in the same room.

Virtuality also seems to balance out participation among members of teams. It is possible that this balancing comes from reduced inhibitions among people who would normally be reluctant to speak up.[17] However, some research suggests that the real balancing factor is the time and effort that it takes to use the technology itself.[18] Most of what we know about participation balancing comes from studies that have relied on email and other text-based virtual communication, so it's unclear whether these patterns hold when people are using video.

Virtual meetings at work can also lead to less emphasis on team members' external characteristics and more emphasis on their work results. In one study, teams in high-virtuality settings were more likely to designate a leader based on achievement, while teams in low-virtuality settings were more likely to designate their leaders based on personality traits or other personal characteristics.[19]

What communication media are best for different types of virtual work?

One of the keys to effective virtual communication is the technology used for interaction. A good way to decide which medium to use for virtual communication is to think about the fit between what needs to be accomplished and the features provided by a given medium. Telephone, email, chat boards, video calls, and file-sharing services each bring advantages and challenges. Effective virtual communicators optimize media use to a given situation and even to the people involved in the situation.[20] While research has identified many factors that can contribute to media optimization, we will focus on three of the most important: (1) the sensitivity of the information being communicated; (2) the complexity of that information; and (3) the urgency of the communication.

What is the best way to communicate sensitive information virtually?

It is best to hold highly sensitive or controversial conversations via a medium that allows participants to share a lot of information. It should also be a medium in which users can interact in real-time. It is also best if such communication takes place using a medium that is difficult to record and share electronically.

One example of a highly sensitive task is terminating an employee. If an in-person conversation is not possible, a video call is nearly always the best choice because participants can see each other's faces and the conversation (in most cases) can only be recorded with the agreement of both parties. Conversely, terminating an employee by email, which initially might feel easier to do, can be harmful to both employee and the employer because the medium conveys limited information, does not allow for immediate questions or clarifications, and can be distributed easily.

In late 2022, Elon Musk laid off thirty-seven hundred employees of the social media company Twitter in one day via email to their personal email addresses, a tactic that raised concerns among government officials and was derided by many human resources professionals as "weak, pathetic, and cruel."[21] Furthermore, because the email firings did not allow for questions or clarifications, the company ended up terminating some employees by mistake, and had to ask them to return several days later.[22] In another case, a Florida restaurant manager fired an employee by email, just twenty minutes after saying goodbye to the employee at the end of a shift. The fired employee quickly posted the email to the online forum Reddit, leading to a viral backlash against the business and coverage of the event in national media.[23] It is easy to imagine how much pain this small business might have avoided if the manager had conducted the firing in person.

What is the best way to communicate complex information virtually?

When communicating sensitive information, the focus is often on emotions and confidentiality. When communicating complex information, however, the focus shifts toward comprehension and accuracy. Because of this, text-based media is often a good way to transmit complex information. For example, while email is not optimal for most sensitive communications, it can be advantageous for communicating complex or nuanced information. First, emails can be drafted carefully and revised, reducing the chances of errors in information transmitted. Second, email allows for many different types of information to be communicated, including text, graphics, and entire files. (However, if complex questions arise about the emailed information, it can still be preferable to hold a call or similar synchronous communication to ensure that doubts are answered quickly and that readers of the email do not become frustrated.)

In some cases, we must handle information virtually that is both sensitive *and* complex or nuanced. One example of this combined setting is virtual negotiations: accuracy is crucial in negotiations, but virtuality can also lead to negative emotions, which can harm negotiations. In this type of situation, the best medium would allow for rich, live interaction as well as text-based communication, such as an integrated video/text platform like Microsoft Teams. One study found that negotiators using richer media were more likely to use collaborative approaches to the negotiation, expressed greater satisfaction with the negotiation, and expressed greater desire for a longer-term negotiating relationship with their partners, as compared with negotiators working over less-rich media.[24]

What is the best way to communicate urgent information virtually?

Finally, it is important to consider the speed with which someone needs to communicate information as part of choosing a virtual medium. For urgent messages or questions, experts generally recommend a medium that is very easy to use, such as telephone or text. One of the reasons that text messaging has become more popular in virtual work settings in the past decade is its speed and relative simplicity. Text messages can often reach recipients long before email, and they are simpler and faster to initiate than telephone or video calls. Texting is particularly useful for messages that are relatively simple or routine and higher in urgency.

3

THE WORKER'S EXPERIENCE
OF REMOTE AND
HYBRID WORK

This chapter will focus primarily on the "remote" aspect of remote work; that is, the physical separation of a worker from their office, supervisor, and co-workers. Virtual communication appears, but as a tool used to facilitate remote work. Three common arrangements defined in the first chapter appear here: working from home, working from anywhere, and hybrid (part-remote, part-in-office) work.

Does remote work help or hurt people's productivity?

This is perhaps the question most frequently asked by managers I've worked with over the years. Before 2020, people often simply assumed that remote work led to lower productivity. After the pandemic lockdowns sent nearly every office worker home, many managers started to develop more-nuanced views. While there is limited research on productivity and remote work up to now, two studies suggest that remote work can result in increased productivity, at least some of the time.

In the first study, a team led by Stanford economist Nicholas Bloom conducted a remote-work experiment at the Chinese travel firm Ctrip, in which some call center agents were allowed to work from home.[1] Productivity among agents in the work-from-home group increased by 13 percent in the nine months of the experiment, and turnover of those employees decreased by 50 percent relative to the control group (which had remained working in the office).

My own research suggests that working from home can also lead to increased worker productivity. Harvard Business School professor Prithwiraj Choudhury, doctoral student Cirrus Foroughi, and I evaluated the impact of a new work-from-anywhere program at the US Patent & Trade Office.[2] Under this program, patent examiners[3] who had already been working from home successfully could opt to shift to an arrangement under which they could live anywhere in the continental United States. The examiners had already experienced some increased productivity when they first shifted from in-office working to working at home (similar to the Chinese call center agents). And yet, we found that the further shift to work from anywhere resulted in an *additional* 4 percent average productivity increase.

This suggests that working from anywhere could potentially provide an additional boost to productivity beyond that of allowing employees to work from home (but still near the office). In fact, it does appear that working from home and working from anywhere influence productivity in different ways. The Chinese call center agents attributed their increased work-from-home productivity to improved work conditions and greater quiet in their home settings. The patent examiners' increased productivity resulted from their expending greater effort on their work. It appears that examiners valued their new geographic flexibility, which increased the overall attractiveness of the job, and thus motivated them to put more effort into their work. Interviews with some of the examiners revealed considerable improvements in their overall lives, such as being able to move closer to extended family, a decreased cost of living, or the ability to live near needed medical care for a child.

Does this mean that all workers will experience increased productivity if moved to work-from-home or work-from-anywhere conditions? Probably not, for two reasons. First, workers in both studies already had a minimum level of *in-office work experience* (six months in the case of the Ctrip agents, and two years for the patent examiners). Second, both customer service and patent examination are highly *independent* types of work; employees need only minimal interactions with other co-workers and supervisors to succeed in their jobs.

Therefore, we might expect increased productivity under remote work for relatively experienced workers (who already know how to do their jobs and have a social network built within their organizations) whose work is relatively independent. For this reason, some firms implementing remote work policies in recent years have focused on experienced workers and independent work—one example of this is Facebook's 2020 announcement that it would allow senior software engineers to work from anywhere.[4]

So, does remote work decrease productivity for all workers who don't fit into these two constraints?

A normal reaction is to wonder what these findings mean for newer employees, and those whose work is less independent and more collaborative. Will these workers suffer from *lower* productivity when working remotely? While there is less empirical research on these types of jobs, most experts believe that while lower productivity is a risk, it is not an inevitability. For these types of jobs, what matters most is the way that employees, their managers, and their companies organize and implement remote work policies and practices.

Are people with a particular type of personality better suited for remote work?

This is another common question about remote work: Are there personality traits that make someone more (or less) capable of working remotely? Research hasn't yet documented consistent links between personality and objectively measured performance while working remotely. However, there are some clues as to what might matter.

Most experts (and most managers that I've consulted with in practice) believe that self-management traits are the most critical for successful remote work. When working remotely, people don't have the benefit of others around them as a check on their behavior. External distractions can be much more tempting outside of the office, requiring remote workers to direct their focus back to their tasks proactively. People who are lower in the trait of conscientiousness are likely to struggle in a remote setting, as they are less likely to be driven to meet deadlines and other expectations.[5] One study found that people with a high tendency for procrastination were more likely to recreationally surf the internet (also known as cyberslacking) and less likely to report that they felt engaged in their work.[6]

Many people assume that introverts—those who need time alone to regain mental energy—would be better suited for remote work. In some ways, that is true. Introverts appear to perform better than extroverts in virtual teamwork, and in some cases report that they feel more comfortable in a remote setting because it meets their need for alone time.[7] But, an open question remains as to whether introverts actually thrive while working remotely over a longer period; their tendency to avoid social settings may lead them to feel isolated.

Another angle on this question is the relationship between personality and attitudes toward (or preference for) remote work. In one 2012 study, researchers found that the personality traits of "agreeableness" (being kind, empathetic, and cooperative with others) and "neuroticism" (being vulnerable to anxiety, stress, and impulsivity) both predicted more positive attitudes toward remote work.[8] These two results may seem contradictory; however, it is actually logical that people who, on one hand, care about pleasing others and wish to be kind (agreeable), but, on the other hand, also find an office setting stressful (neurotic) could express a preference for remote work.

Personality does not guarantee success (or failure). People without these traits can still be highly successful at remote work; it may just take a bit more effort. Regardless of personality, success requires the development and practice of remote work skills, just as with any other activity.

Are there gender or racial/ethnic differences in people's preferences for remote work?

Many people—researchers included—start with a baseline assumption that women with school-aged children are more likely to prefer working from home. But this is a simplistic view, and it's important to separate the effect of gender from that of childrearing. And findings about women's preferences somewhat mirror those of other underrepresented groups, a parallel that became much more apparent during the pandemic.

First, gender: most surveys over the past thirty years report that women do report a higher overall preference for remote work, with few exceptions. (These exceptions may relate in part to location: one Dutch study found no significant differences between women and men.[9])

Evidence for the effect of childrearing responsibility is less clear. One factor that often predicts a desire to *not* work remotely is having a large household (i.e., many children or other dependents living at home).[10] But one

1993 study found the opposite, with strongest preferences held by people with more than two children under the age of sixteen at home.[11] A McKinsey survey in early 2021 (while some pandemic restrictions were still in place) reported that both men and women with small children had stronger preferences for remote work. But another survey commissioned by Harvard Business School around the same time found that parents with children at home wanted to go back to the office full-time more than other workers.[12]

It is possible that women's preference for remote work goes beyond simply childcare. A 2012 survey of university professors found that women were more likely to mention work-related reasons (such as increased productivity) than family-related reasons (such as childcare) for preferring flexible work arrangements.[13] Women may find remote work more productive in part because of the gender-related challenges they often face in the workplace. On average, women spend considerably more time and money than men on grooming and dressing for work, and research suggests that they must do so to succeed professionally.[14] Women also are more likely to face greater judgment and are at a greater risk of sexual harassment in the workplace, and even more so in male-dominated organizations.[15]

In fact, a similar theme—reducing harmful in-office dynamics—has been found in many first-person accounts and surveys of people of color and LGBTQ+ orientations since the beginning of the COVID pandemic. Many employees from these communities report that they have discovered that remote work allows them to focus on their work, without being constantly reminded of their differences from others in the workplace, or having to tolerate microaggressions or well-meaning but inappropriate comments from co-workers. In a *New York Times* article, Julia McCluney, an assistant professor at Cornell, described common microaggressions for Black women as often occurring in person: "Things like having your hair touched or people commenting on your body, or asking 'Oh what are you eating? It smells weird. . . . This is why we don't all want to go back into the office."[16]

Reducing perceived differences is also easier in a remote setting. In a *Los Angeles Times* opinion piece, Eugene S. Robinson, a Black animation studio owner, described preparing for a client call by removing his beanie, exchanging a Black Panther pajama top for a shirt, and putting on a pair of (non-prescription) horn-rimmed glasses to arrive at his "make-people comfortable outfit." Robinson, himself a Black male executive noted, "Telework came to the rescue. In real life I am 6-foot-1 and 220 pounds. On a Zoom call, I am about an inch tall and just as wide across. Physicality: gone. . . . Is this what a meritocratic work experience feels like?"[17]

A Harris poll found that 63 percent of Black workers and 58 percent of (all) women reported feeling more ambitious when working remotely than when working in the office. In an *Axios* story about the poll, John Gerzema, CEO of the Harris Poll, noted these statistics, saying, "It's output over office politics. It's the theater of the office that is often alienating women workers, workers of color, women of color."[18]

Are there generational or age differences in people's preference for remote work?

We don't know much about age-based preferences for remote work prior to the pandemic. One very early study based on data from 1992 found that older workers were less likely to prefer remote work.[19] But another study in 1999 found no significant differences among age groups for levels of remote work.[20] (Few participants in that study were not allowed to work remotely by employers; therefore, it is safe to assume that their actual amounts of remote work were a good proxy for preferences).

Coming out of the pandemic in 2022, there do seem to be some clear age-related trends. A 2022 McKinsey survey showed that younger workers (ages eighteen to twenty-four) are more likely to have the opportunity to work remotely and are likely to look for another job if not given the option to do so. And yet, when they can work remotely, they actually do so on average *fewer* days per week than any other age group.[21] This makes sense because younger adults are more likely to be single and childless and are thus looking for more social interaction outside the home. Furthermore, as they are early in their careers, they are typically also more interested in learning from others as well as networking with others at work. They're also often sharing their living spaces with roommates, making remote work more difficult.

Similarly, it makes sense that the age group most interested in remote work are those in the twenty-five to forty age range. This group of workers is more settled professionally and socially, and often contending with the greatest levels of childrearing responsibility. According to an Axios Harris 100 poll in 2022, 84 percent of this age group expressed a preference for remote work, as compared with 66 percent of their younger counterparts.[22]

The picture becomes fuzzier for older age groups. Surveys from 2022 indicate that workers in both the forty-one to fifty-five and fifty-six to seventy age groups have strong preferences for—and actual amounts of—remote work, although this seems to diminish a bit over time.[23] Some of the decreased preference and remote work among older people is likely due to their relative seniority in their organizations; in general, more senior managers feel more pressure to be present in the office. But we don't know yet whether some of this difference among older workers' preferences is simply a generational difference that will disappear in another decade, or if there is something related to in-office work that appeals more to people who are likely to have grown children and fewer responsibilities at home.

Are there other factors that cause people to prefer remote work?

The most consistent predictor of desire to work remotely appears to be the amount of time it takes an employee to commute to and from the office. The average commute time one-way in the United States in 2019 was 27.6 minutes, according to the US Census Bureau.[24] This time represents close to five hours per workweek spent simply getting to and from the office. And this time is an average, which means that many people (especially in larger metro areas with limited public transit) spend considerably more time and money on their commutes.

The relationship between commute time and preference for remote work appears to hold true in other countries as well. One recent study showed that participants residing in both the United States and India exhibited similar links between commute time and preference for remote work.[25] Dutch workers surveyed in 2004 also reported a higher preference for remote work when commute time was longer.[26]

Do remote workers feel isolated from others?

Isolation is one of the most common negative side effects of remote work. In fact, the isolation and loneliness among workers confined to their homes appear to have been a factor in the spike in mental-health challenges during the pandemic.[27] The early pandemic period was obviously an extreme setting in which people were isolated both in and out of work hours, but the effects of that isolation point to the potential for similar challenges for remote workers in more normal times. Supporting this, when workers in Bloom's study of Chinese call center agents had the opportunity to return to the office, those who chose to return were most likely to cite loneliness as the deciding factor.[28]

As we've already discussed, people who generally prefer being alone are less likely to feel isolated when working remotely.[29] Conversely, people who engage in relationship-building proactively experience less isolation when working remotely because they are driven to reach out to others, even when the others are not physically present.[30] And of course, people with family at home during the day are less likely to report feeling isolated (and may occasionally wish for more isolation!).

But young people are highly vulnerable to feeling isolated when working remotely. One junior manager whom I interviewed during the height of the pandemic was single and lived alone. She said that normally she was a fairly independent person and enjoyed living alone, but she reported feeling some despair upon realizing that she had not spoken out loud about anything other than work for several days, and she had not seen anyone in person for even longer. Even after pandemic restrictions were lifted, I heard from recently graduated former students that they felt "trapped and alone," as one described it, working in all-remote jobs with little opportunity to professionally network or informally socialize with their co-workers. One former student reported, "I was really psyched at first when I realized that I could roll out of bed 15 minutes before work started, but after a few weeks, that became old, and the job became lonely and boring."

How do remote workers avoid feelings of isolation?

Up to now, there has been little research on what people can do themselves to feel less isolated. However, a range of practices has begun to emerge over the last few years.

The most skilled remote workers that I have observed find ways to incorporate a variety of interactions into their schedules. These interactions typically span *work and non-work hours*, include *work and non-work content*, and involve both *in-person and virtual interactions*. I often recommend that people consider the eight possible combinations of these three dimensions and estimate how much of their daily interactions fall within each. Many times when someone feels isolated or lonely in remote work, it is either because they have very few daily interactions of any type, or because most of their interactions occur in work hours, involve work content, and are virtual. In these cases, it can be helpful to seek out and plan for opportunities that fall outside of this category.

There are simple ways to increase interaction during the workday and virtually that do not involve work content. For instance, joining an online Employee Resource Group or other employee interest group can help people to build non-work interactions and find shared interests with co-workers. Many people find ways to chat informally with their work friends, whether via text, phone, or a chat application such as Slack or Yammer.

Importantly, interaction does not have to take place just with co-workers, even during the workday; it could be with members of a lunchtime exercise class, a neighbor, or even a (preferably adult) family member. Some people find that working in a coffee shop for a few hours a day helps them feel more connected to their community while giving them a change of scenery. A common sentiment about coffee-shop working was expressed on the online discussion board Quora by Dallas-based manager Blythe

Renay: "Working in isolation can be really lonely! And sometimes you just want a little murmur of conversation in the background. That sort of thing helps me to focus sometimes!"[31] Entrepreneur Vivek Nair noted, "The effect is similar to working with your teammates in a physical office without the other silly office optics."[32]

What impact does working remotely have on work–life balance?

The effect of remote work on home life and work–life balance is sometimes described as a paradox. Having the flexibility to work from home can reduce the extent to which work impinges on our personal lives, also called "work–family conflict."[33] It can mean employees are available for family activities earlier in the evening, or to take a child to a dentist appointment. But remote work can also *increase* levels of "family–work conflict," the impingement of family on work life.[34] This increase is particularly notable at higher levels of remote work. For example, if a parent is working remotely full-time, they may find themselves under more pressure to take on household errands during the workday than someone who only works from home one or two days per week. The net impact of increased family–work conflict and decreased work–family conflict varies for different people and situations. For this reason, there is no clear relationship between remote work and overall work–life balance.[35]

If anything, the net effect of remote work on work–life balance appears to be a blurring of the boundaries between work and personal lives, with increased connectivity to work at all hours leading to increased pressure to work longer.[36] Because of this blurring, managing boundaries has become an important skill for remote workers.

People can manage boundaries by setting—and enforcing—expectations about times for work, both with family and with work colleagues. Another strategy used by some is to engage in a specific ritual to signal (to themselves and others) the beginning and end of a workday. For instance, one financial professional who worked remotely for years before COVID-19 would dress in full work clothes (in her firm's case, a suit) before entering her home office; this signaled to both her and her young children that it was work time.

Many people find actions as simple as closing a laptop or pouring a glass of wine at the end of the day to be useful reminders to themselves that the workday is over, and that it is time to focus on other aspects of their lives. For those working in tight spaces, a long-time remote worker suggests keeping a "work bag" in which laptop and papers go at the end of the day.[37] One of my favorite—albeit extreme—examples of boundary management during the height of the COVID-19 pandemic was that of a young professional living in a small studio apartment who would sit at one end of their sofa each day to work on their laptop, and then signal the end of the day by moving to the other end of the sofa and turning on the television.

Is there any such thing as an ideal amount of remote work?

You may have gathered from some of the earlier answers in this chapter that while there are a lot of benefits to remote work, more is not always better. Tim Golden, a professor at Rensselaer Polytechnic Institute, has documented this phenomenon in a series of studies showing that there is often an inverted U-shaped relationship between the extent of remote work and outcomes such as performance and job satisfaction.

One of these studies suggests that remote work is associated with increased job satisfaction up to about 15 hours per week; the effects then plateau, and ultimately decline at higher levels of remote work. While this finding only documents an association, not a cause-and-effect relationship, it suggests that there may be an optimal level for job satisfaction around two days per week of remote work.

Golden conducted his studies before the pandemic, so it is unclear whether this optimal amount of remote work may have shifted, given that we now enjoy better communications technology and are more skilled at maintaining remote relationships. However, more recent surveys of worker desires for remote work are not far from Golden's original findings, with a typical average ideal of between two and three remote days per week.[38]

Does working remotely hurt people's career advancement?

People who work remotely most or all the time often wonder whether the adage "out of sight, out of mind" applies to them, and whether co-workers who spend more time in the office are more likely to be promoted, regardless of work performance. There is some evidence to support these fears. For example, Nick Bloom's study of Chinese call center agents found that, despite increased productivity, lower absenteeism, and lower attrition rates, remote workers received significantly fewer promotions as compared to those in the office.[39] A 2021 survey of supervisors of remote workers showed that 67 percent of responding managers admitted that they viewed remote workers as more dispensable than in-office workers, and 62 percent said they believed that remote work was detrimental to career progression.[40] These disparities may lessen in the future, as most people now have worked remotely and many promoting managers are themselves still working remotely. But my post-pandemic consulting and executive education experiences suggest anecdotally that career progression continues to be a major concern. Regardless of future trends, there are specific steps that people can take to increase their social presence and remain top-of-mind when promotion opportunities arise.

What actions can help increase the odds of getting noticed, and promoted, while working remotely?

Many experts believe the two main causes of remote workers' promotion challenges are proximity bias and reduced networking opportunities. Proximity bias refers to a tendency to prefer things that are physically closer to those that are not. In recent years, the term has been used to describe supervisors' apparent preference for in-office workers versus remote workers. The presence of this bias highlights the importance of remote workers establishing and maintaining a virtual presence when they are not in the office.

Maintaining a strong virtual presence requires more intentional effort than a similar in-office physical presence. In-office employees have presence simply by showing up. Remotely, a person must create their virtual presence. One of the simplest ways that people create a virtual presence at work is to use video (as appropriate) as much as possible. We previously discussed the role of video in lowering construal levels and lessening fundamental attribution error—these effects help create a positive virtual presence just as they reduce the odds of misunderstanding in communication.

A second, related strategy is for the employee to consider the image they are portraying on video at least as carefully as they would in the office. In the office, the main consideration for an employee is their own appearance (dress and grooming). In a remote setting, employee image also benefits from a professional (or at least non-distracting) background, a stable internet connection, and comfort in using and troubleshooting communication technology.

Finally, much advice about maintaining a virtual presence relates to the idea of proactivity at work. Speaking up in meetings, volunteering for new projects, and initiating improvements to one's own work without being asked are great ways to promote and maintain a virtual presence. Proactive employees in general have stronger career trajectories.[41] This likely holds true in remote settings as well. And proactivity does not have to be all work-related. Some of the steps that help to reduce isolation while working remotely—such as participating in an employee group or club—also work to increase virtual presence.

Proactivity is also critical in overcoming a lack of networking opportunities. Successful remote workers take the initiative in (virtually) approaching senior executives, peers in other parts of the organization, and even subordinates they might not know. Networking outreach is most effective when it includes offers of help or information or involves a simple request for fifteen to twenty minutes on video conference to learn more about the network contact's own work and career. As consultant Duncan Wardle noted in the *Harvard Business Review*, "One thing about networking that will never change is that executives generally like to talk about themselves."[42]

Some younger professionals have found that increased remote work opens up new opportunities for networking and mentorship. Because senior executives are spending less time traveling, and more time working remotely themselves, they are sometimes more willing to engage in virtual relationship building than they would have been pre-pandemic. A 2022 *Wall Street Journal* article described thirty-year-old endocrinology fellow Priya Jaisinghani's remote mentoring relationship with Vineet Arora, the dean for medical education at the University of Chicago Pritzker

School of Medicine. Despite initial reservations about remote mentoring, Arora responded to Jaisinghani's initial
outreach because of Jaisinghani's enthusiasm for specific
aspects of Arora's work. The two ended up collaborating
on a research project and building a rewarding mentoring
relationship despite not having met in person.[43]

How is the experience of hybrid work different from that of all-remote work?

Hybrid work is simply a combination of remote and in-
office work and, as such, defines everyone who works part
(but not all) of the time out of the office. The biggest advantage of hybrid work is that it allows for optimization
between the two settings—if well managed, people can
enjoy the increased flexibility of some remote work days,
while also enjoying the increased networking and learning
opportunities and reduced isolation of the office.

However, the extent to which someone can actually
achieve this optimization depends a great deal on how
well the hybrid environment is set up and operated, by
managers, work teams, and the organization itself. If hybrid work is not well run, the result for the worker can be
both enormous frustration and poor performance.

4

MANAGERS: SUPERVISING REMOTE WORKERS AND MANAGING REMOTELY

As much as individual workers experience challenges in remote work, managers have an arguably even greater hurdle; they need to ensure both performance from and stability for people they cannot see. This chapter will focus on the most important factors of remote supervision and management, whether as a formal boss or as an individual responsible for ensuring that a workflow is completed by remote others.

In a 2002 paper about virtual teams, Brad Bell and Steve Kozlowski of Michigan State University predicted that effective managers would need to "create infrastructures" for dispersed employees, to enable activities ranging from information sharing to decision-making to conflict resolution.[1] Infrastructure is a useful way to think about how managers (and companies) keep their remote workers connected and motivated. The infrastructure required for effective remote work includes new behaviors and routines, as well as technological infrastructure.

How do managers of remote workers know that their employees are actually doing their jobs?

The abrupt transition to remote work in 2020 struck fear into many managers, who were suddenly leading remote workers for the first time. Much of this fear stemmed from their lack of trust in their employees to remain productive outside of the office. In the summer of 2020, *Harvard Business Review* published an article in which researchers surveyed 215 remote managers in twenty-four countries, and found that thirty-eight percent agreed with the statement that remote workers perform worse than those working in an office, and that another twenty-two percent were unsure.[2] While 2020 is an extreme example, it illustrates struggles that I have observed among managers who are newly charged with ensuring performance and productivity from a remote workforce.

Despite these statistics, managers have been supervising remote workforces successfully for years, and their experiences point to some key success factors. The first of these is perhaps the most important: people should manage using output-based performance objectives, rather than presence-based evaluation. One of the biggest mistakes that managers make in general—remote or in the office—is to evaluate employee performance based on observed effort rather than actual results.

A few years ago, I worked with a financial services company that had made a (well-founded) strategic decision to convert most of its back-office workforce to remote or hybrid work. However, quite a few of the managers were expressing discomfort with the idea of remote supervision. I ran a workshop with a group of senior managers in which I challenged each manager to choose one subordinate. I asked the managers to write down all the ways that the employee's work added value to the organization as a basis for how they might evaluate the employee's remote performance. The list could include quantitative or qualitative measures of output, but it needed to be specific. As I began to debrief this exercise, one manager's example came to the forefront, in part because he picked a long-time employee known by many in the group.

Even though the employee was well known and liked, neither her manager nor anyone else in the group could clearly define what her work was, or what it contributed to the overall business. I tried asking clarifying questions to get at the answer, and kept hearing replies along the lines of, "She works really hard; I know what she does is important."

My point here is not that this person's job was superfluous; it is quite likely that her work was essential to the organization. But the fact that no one was able to explain that work or its impact on the organization meant that it was impossible to evaluate her performance on anything other than her physical presence and perceived effort.

What can managers do to help improve performance among remote employees?

In 2023, the *Annual Review of Organizational Psychology and Organizational Behavior* published a synthesis of decades of research on leaders of virtual and remote teams and employees.[3] The paper outlined four functions that are particularly important for managers of remote workers. First, strong virtual leaders "encourage self-management," meaning that they both give employees some autonomy over their work and also encourage employees to use that autonomy proactively to help make key decisions, to make sure that work is progressing, and to ask for help and feedback. Second, managers very clearly set out expectations and goals—this needs to be a much more transparent, intentional process than in an office setting because remote employees are unable to sense "shifting winds" related to a project the way that they can in the office.

Third, effective managers of remote workers spend time developing good social relationships with their

employees, as well as supporting relationship development among remote employees. This again requires attention to a dynamic that often occurs organically in the
office. And finally, these managers must make technology
use an active part of their overall strategy by ensuring
appropriate technology is available, establishing norms
for its use, and adapting technology to changing needs
over time.

As we look at some of the best practices of effective
managers in the remainder of this chapter, we will see
these themes of autonomy, connection, norm-setting, and
technology use appear and often overlap each other.

How do managers keep remote workers connected and motivated?

Raghu Krishnamoorthy, University of Pennsylvania
Fellow and a former chief human resources officer of
General Electric, differentiates between the less effective
practice of micromanagement and a set of practices that
he calls "microunderstanding."[4] Managers engaging in
microunderstanding have an integrated, consistent presence in remote employees' workdays, but with a focus on
support rather than monitoring. One study participant il-
lustrated this practice by noting, "My boss has amped up
the operating mechanisms over the last few months; we
have regular meetings whereby we go over our goals, our
accomplishments, and gaps on a frequent basis so that we
are all aligned as to what needs to be done. It has lent a
level of predictability and consistency to our world—
necessary, since we do not have easy real-time connections
anymore."[5]

This quote points to two key components of
Krishnamoorthy's practice of microunderstanding: (1)
keeping remote employees *aware of the broader context* in

which their work takes place; and (2) maintaining consistent and predictable *routines of communication*.

Why is it important for remote workers to know about their organizations beyond their specific jobs?

It is easy for remote employees to lose sight of how their work fits into and influences the organization's overall outcomes. (As used here, the term "organization" could mean a department, a business unit, or the entire company.) This is another form of the "situational information" and situational awareness mentioned previously. Just as with interpersonal situational information, employees' awareness of the broader work environment tends to be reduced in a remote work setting, and one of the key roles of managers is to build and maintain this awareness intentionally.

Regular updates help keep remote employees aware of the overall business landscape. These updates ensure that employees have a common understanding of short-term challenges and goals, as well as longer-term strategic aims. Managers can use periodic work group or team meetings to ensure a common understanding of the work environment among employees and to allow for questions and discussion.

As important as it is for employees to understand the business, they must also understand the impact and importance of their work to remain motivated and connected to the organization. Understanding the specific impact of one's work on other people—whether clients or coworkers—is critical for motivating all employees, whether remote or in-office.[6] Yet managers sometimes forget to communicate this to employees, especially those who are not physically nearby.

A simple way for managers to think about maintaining awareness among remote employees is to ensure they are communicating the answers to two questions on an ongoing basis: What is going on in our work group and in the organization? And how is (the employee's) work contributing to our work group and to the organization?

What is a communication routine and how does it help remote employees?

Establishing and maintaining a predictable communication routine is crucial to managing remote employees effectively. A communication routine includes both the frequency and rhythm of communication, as well as the medium used for communication. A typical communication routine between a manager and employee could be, "We have one-on-one updates at 9 am on Tuesday and Friday mornings for about 20 minutes, and there is a weekly all-hands department meeting on Wednesday afternoons at 4 pm. These meetings are held on video."

Managers' communication routines should include regular one-on-one conversations with all their remote subordinates. Scheduling, and holding, regular meetings with each remote employee requires more effort than in-office supervision and can feel time-consuming. Yet this practice yields extensive dividends by improving the quality of supervisor–employee relationships.[7] One-on-one conversations help remote employees feel visible (and their absence often makes employees feel forgotten); as such, they are an important tool in maintaining motivation and connection.

Communication routines may vary depending on the employee and their work. A new or struggling employee will likely need more frequent communication, as well as a richer medium (e.g., brief daily check-in meetings via videoconference). A highly experienced and proactive employee who is thriving in a remote setting may only need to join a department all-hands meeting once a week, with one-on-one calls once or twice each month. I recently employed a temporary research associate who lived in another state. We started with almost-daily one-on-one check-ins when she first began the job. After a couple of weeks, we changed our check-ins to two times per week. As part of this transition, we discussed and agreed on the frequency and days that we would hold these meetings. By the end of her contract period, she was working very autonomously and communicating frequently with the full research team; as a result, we sometimes met only once per week.

Managers typically also ensure that communication routines help to build relationships and community among co-workers by including opportunities for peer connection. Ideally, these opportunities include a mix of virtual and in-person connections. One common practice is for managers to start online meetings with a few minutes of non-work conversation. Intentionally leaving time for social interaction helps employees to know each other, makes them more likely to give each other the benefit of the doubt (by avoiding fundamental attribution error), and builds trust and cohesion in a team.

What else can managers do to maintain relationships with and among remote employees?

Effective managers create opportunities wherever possible for at least occasional in-person interactions among their employees. Research has consistently shown that even minimal face-to-face interaction—especially interaction that contains a relationship-building component—is a wise *business* investment because it leads to much faster development of trust and cohesion, and more efficient subsequent communication among employees.[8]

Managers of hybrid teams can ensure face-to-face interaction relatively easily, by scheduling at least one "all-hands" day in the office each week, when all employees come into the office. However, scheduling alone is not sufficient. Managers must then plan activities for that day which take advantage of employees' physical co-location. These activities should include a mix of work (ideally the work that requires the greatest level of collaboration or complex discussion) and social interaction. A manager's typical weekly all-hands schedule might include a group or team meeting in the morning, followed by one-on-one meetings with direct reports, a work group lunch, and then time for small-group collaboration in the afternoon.

Arranging in-person interaction can be more complicated for managers of all-remote employees. It is critical to view remote workers' in-person visits to the office as an important investment in the business itself. Experienced managers tend to arrange opportunities for remote employees to come into the office, but the frequency varies widely, depending on both the role and the location of the employee. An employee undertaking easily measurable, transactional, and mostly independent work (e.g., a customer service agent for a bank) could come into the office to re-connect with others only once per year. In contrast, an employee whose work involves high amounts of collaboration, uncertainty, and complexity (e.g., a product development manager) might come in as frequently as once a month.

How do managers support remote workers who are feeling lonely or isolated?

Feelings of loneliness and isolation can be a serious downside of remote work, especially for workers who rarely go into the office. Managers have a critical role in monitoring for signs of isolation, as well as helping employees find ways to manage these feelings.

Regular conversations are an ideal starting point, as they enable managers to evaluate employees' state of mind better than with a work group conference call. But this does not come naturally to all managers. Managers who are accustomed to sticking to task-related conversations often resist asking about their employees' feelings. But ignoring emotions and relationships has been associated with lower employee job satisfaction, motivation, and higher levels of burnout.[9]

Another reason managers often avoid conversations about feelings with employees is that they are afraid that by doing so they will give the employee a reason to slack off or reduce their performance. Even in person, many managers struggle to maintain a balance between building supportive personal relationships with employees while also pushing them to perform. This struggle can be even more challenging in a remote work setting, as managers cannot observe employees (as they would in the office) to gauge their level of well-being or their productivity.

Managers need to recognize that poor job performance often is a *result* of feelings of isolation or loneliness, as employees feel disconnected from the organization and even from the purpose of their jobs. Work-based social support can be the factor that brings the remote employee back into the fold, increasing their connection with the organization.[10]

The best way to assess employees' state of mind is simply to ask, early and often. Making a well-being check-in part of the regular conversation between manager and employee makes it more comfortable than a one-off, unexpected inquiry that may feel intrusive and leave the employee feeling concerned about their job security ("why is she asking me this now?")

One of the best examples I have found of unobtrusive well-being checks comes from an ongoing study of long-haul truck drivers. Through a series of interviews, I found a range of communication patterns between supervisors and drivers. Managers who sustained longer-term relationships with their drivers typically engaged in repeated, short check-ins with their drivers, and these check-ins typically included some sort of well-being inquiry. For long-haul truck drivers, well-being is a considerable challenge because drivers can be isolated, not only from co-workers but also from their families.

The driver supervisors' inquiries are deliberately low-key, so that drivers feel free to discuss areas of personal concern or can simply report that all is well. A typical inquiry (as reported to me in the interviews) could be simply, "How are you doing today?" One supervisor said that he always asks drivers, "How did you wake up this morning?" which is light in tone but also gives the driver an opening to report if they have been worried or upset about something.

For remote workers, feelings of loneliness and isolation vary dramatically by individual. Some people enjoy the solitude of remote work and may chafe at regular check-ins, while others will need considerable support. As with all other remote communication, managers typically work out norms for regular check-ins, often after a period of experimenting with different options.

How do managers ensure that remote workers have career-progression opportunities?

Remote workers face career challenges related to overcoming proximity bias among managers; that is, the tendency to think more positively about employees who are physically nearby. This bias is also a challenge for managers, in that they are less likely to choose the best candidates for promotion if they fall victim to proximity bias. So, ensuring remote workers have equal career progression opportunities is as much about running a strong business as it is about supporting individual workers.

Earlier in this chapter, I mentioned the case of the manager who could not identify what their employee did, even though they had observed her working very hard for years. This type of realization has been widespread since the beginning of the COVID-19 pandemic, and it demonstrates how much managers have relied on physical presence as an indicator of performance. It is clear that a manager oriented toward physical presence would then view a remote employee as a lower performer than an employee in the office. Such a manager is also likely to overestimate their in-office employee's performance.

Successful managers evaluate employee performance based on specific goals, rather than physical presence. Goals can be quantitative (e.g., number of calls completed, dollars of revenue earned) or they can be more qualitative (e.g., completion of high-quality marketing plan by deadline). Goals should also be updated regularly and are often used as the basis of conversation in periodic one-on-one calls.

Including one-on-one update meetings with remote employees in communication routines is critical to enabling equal access for those employees. Similarly, managers should hold meetings involving remote and in-office employees entirely on a digital platform (with in-office employees joining from their desks), rather than gathering some employees in a conference room and digitally bringing in others.

When considering both remote and in-office candidates for high-profile projects or promotion opportunities, managers should check for proximity bias by writing down lists of what they know about each candidate's

accomplishments, strengths, and areas needing development. If they find that they struggle to complete the lists
more for remote candidates than for in-office candidates,
it is likely that they will be more vulnerable to proximity
bias. One way to remedy this gap is to gather information
on a remote employee from a variety of sources; another is
simply to be aware of the risk of proximity bias to ensure
that decision-making is based on complete information.

How does a manager replicate informal chats that occur when stopping by an employee's desk?

This question is a good place to mention one communication practice that does not keep remote employees
motivated or connected. Some of the managers who
struggle the most with the transition to remote supervision are those who were accustomed to the "managing by
wandering around" approach popularized by the book *In
Search of Excellence* in the late twentieth century.[11] A manager who supervises this way spends time during the day
checking in with employees by walking through the areas
where they are working and chatting with them informally.

For managers who have used this strategy successfully for years, scheduling a regular cadence of remote
communication routines can feel stilted or robotic at first.
However, in my experience, most of these managers find
that once they establish a routine of regular one-on-one
meetings with their remote employees (usually once or
twice per week), they are able to provide the same support
and connection.

However, sometimes managers have used desk visits
in the office as a form of monitoring, and as a substitute
for trusting their employees. If a manager's previous wandering around involved more status requests ("what are
you working on?") and fewer offers of problem-solving

and support ("do you need anything from me?"), it is likely that the mangers were using the strategy for monitoring, and that the manager will struggle more to adapt to a remote work setting.[12]

I have worked with managers who initially tried to replicate desk visits by digitally "wandering around," often by checking in on employees via the company chat function, by text, or sometimes by phone call. In these cases, if the employee did not reply quickly, the manager often would escalate the communication from check-in to real monitoring, with an inquiry along the lines of "where are you?"

These types of inquiries can be appropriate in a few situations: if there is a truly urgent situation at hand, or if a subordinate is missing a meeting or has been missing in action for an extended time. But if managers use these check-ins regularly with responsible employees, they can be extremely demotivating. I have heard employees on the receiving end of these message describe them as "bed checks," referring to camp counselors taking inventory of their charges. This term accurately reflects the infantilizing effect of trying to monitor employees remotely by constantly checking in.

For managers who truly do just want to connect informally to offer support, a simple tactic is a message clearly stating that the manager is available if needed, but that an immediate reply is not expected. An example of such a message might be, "Hi there, I know you're working hard on [project]. No reply needed, but don't hesitate to reach out if you feel like you're hitting any roadblocks—I'm happy to help."

How do managers of remote workers give effective feedback?

There is really not much difference between giving feedback in a remote setting and doing it face-to-face. But, as with many other aspects of management, remoteness can highlight or exacerbate ineffective feedback practices. Managers need to ensure that they are engaging in healthy feedback conversations, giving specific examples of behaviors and results, and treating feedback as a mutual conversation with the employee rather than a one-way flow of information to the employee. Two feedback practices are particularly critical to get right in a remote setting: (1) delivering feedback personally; and (2) optimizing the frequency of feedback.

Effective remote managers typically hold feedback conversations on a medium that conveys a lot of information, such as a video call. Sending developmental feedback via email, for example, can cause it to seem more threatening or intimidating than intended and employees are more likely to misinterpret the message. Sending a carefully crafted email with positive feedback is wonderful; but, combining that with in-person praise can have even more impact.

There are benefits to putting both positive and constructive feedback in writing—it provides a permanent point of reference for both the giver and the recipient. But limiting feedback to written communication limits its benefits. Think about how you would feel if you were working in an office and your manager (also in the office) sent you an email with feedback, without saying anything to you about it. In an office setting, that would feel strange, and even a little hostile. The same effects occur in a remote setting, but managers are more likely to convince themselves that only written feedback is sufficient because of the remoteness (while employees still feel the absence of a live conversation).

If a manager is only giving an employee feedback once or twice a year, as part of a formal review process, they are not effectively developing that employee. This is true whether the employee is remote or in the office every day. But there is also such a thing as too much feedback—very frequent feedback can become distracting and can hurt employee performance.[13] The manager's job is to find the optimal level of feedback that allows employees to maximize their performance and learning. This is particularly important in a remote setting, as too much feedback can leave employees feeling micromanaged, while too little feedback can leave employees feeling abandoned and forgotten. As with all other communication norms that we have covered in this chapter, it is best to agree on—and then follow—a frequency for informal feedback with each remote employee.

How does a manager working remotely supervise in-office subordinates effectively?

Even before the COVID-19 pandemic, it was common to find managers who worked remotely supervising in-office employees. While much of what we have already covered applies to this type of situation, there are two additional dynamics that merit some attention: dealing with tensions stemming from perceived inequity and ensuring virtual presence and availability to employees.

A manager allowed to supervise from afar can be the source of resentment among employees who are required to work in the office. When the employees' jobs could be performed remotely but the employees are not allowed to do so, the resentment is even more intense because employees perceive unfairness in their work arrangement. Tensions related to perceived inequity between managers and employees' remote work allowances have become more systematic, and more intense, since the COVID-19 pandemic and have extended to differences between senior and middle managers. In late 2022, one executive search firm reported that 80 percent of their open positions (director through C-suite levels) were available to remote employees.[14] Around the same time, a survey by consultancy Future Forum reported that senior executives were almost twice as likely as middle managers to report few constraints on their work schedules, and three times more likely to report no work schedule constraints.[15] And yet, it is senior executives who also express a strong desire for their employees to return to the office. When employees perceive inequity, they are typically less motivated and often reduce the effort they put into their work.[16]

Managers who work remotely should consider whether they could extend the same privilege to their employees. If this is not feasible, then managers should at a minimum acknowledge the difference to their employees and lay out specific steps that they (the manager) will take to ensure that they are as available and communicative with employees virtually as they would be if they were in the office.

In 2020, I wrote for *Harvard Business Review* about a conversation I had with Mark Strassman, who then worked as a senior executive for the technology firm Logmein.[17] Strassman was based in California, while Logmein headquarters and much of his two-thousand-person business unit were based in Boston. To increase his availability to employees and lessen the burden of multiple meetings, Strassman held a weekly virtual office hour to which all his employees were invited. Because Strassman's employees were spread across time zones, he varied the times of the office hour each week.

The office hours allowed Strassman to speak informally with a range of employees and address any urgent topics. The sessions also reduced the number of thirty-minute meetings put on his calendar during the week because employees learned that many issues could be resolved during office hours in five minutes or less. Finally, Strassman reported that office hours also provided an additional opportunity for employees from different parts of his organization to connect with each other, as well as with him.

How do managers of remote workers manage to get their own work done and prevent exhaustion and burnout?

Remote work requires a lot of additional communication from managers. This can be frustrating. In a workshop I ran recently, one executive sighed with exasperation and said, "I hate remote work. I have to do so much more than I ever did before, and I am exhausted. And nothing is working as well as it used to." In fact, some academics I talk to have begun to question whether managers of remote workers experience a greater impact professionally and psychologically from the remoteness than do the employees they supervise. A few observations can help those who are feeling this frustration.

First, remote management generally gets easier and more efficient over time. The managers themselves must come up a learning curve; remote management requires new behaviors and practices, and it also reduces the number of managerial shortcuts they can take. It takes a period of experimentation to get to the optimal communication routines and practices. No one chooses the perfect set of practices on the first try; there are always employees who need a little more or a little less, technology norms that can be improved, and new ways to build community among co-workers. Experienced managers find that a huge amount of learning occurs as a result of initial discomfort or failure.

Managers also need to accept that remote management is fundamentally different from in-office management and that they need to do real work to develop new practices and habits. For more experienced in-office managers, the shift to remote can mean that they need to discard practices that have worked for them in the past, and perhaps have even been the root of their success as managers. Both academics and business journalists have wondered aloud whether some of the resistance to long-term remote work among senior executives stems from their own desire to stick with tried-and-true leadership behaviors, rather than adapt to a new environment.[18]

Finally, managers of remote workers should look for ways to use the flexibility inherent in remote management to improve their own work lives. One example of this is a practice, taken up by many managers during the pandemic, of going for long walks while holding less complex work calls. Managers might also combine travel to client sites with visits to remote employees (at a coffee shop or other public location). The most successful managers find ways to make the most of the benefits of remoteness while also working through the challenges.

5

WORKING EFFECTIVELY
IN REMOTE TEAMS

The word "team" is used loosely in many work environments to refer to groups of people reporting to the same manager. Sometimes a team is a department. But a true work team is a group of people working together toward a shared goal.[1] It is this coordinated work that makes teams both powerful and difficult; high-performing teams must not only get their tasks done, but they also have to develop a process for working together, along with a reasonable amount of trust and social cohesion. All of this is difficult in any circumstance (see athletic teams, for example). But when team members are in different places the challenges become even greater.

Geographically dispersed teams have been around much longer than remote workers due in part to the growth of multinational corporations and the increase in outsourcing. Because of this, much of the early research findings on virtual and remote work came from studying teams, rather than individual people.[2] In this chapter, we will look at two different kinds of geographically distributed teams and examine the practices that are associated with high performance.

One word of caution: even though there are several decades' worth of research on remote teams, much of this work is on teams of university students (in laboratories and in classes) rather than real teams in organizations. Two analyses in recent years have demonstrated that findings in certain areas—such as team leadership and culture—can vary depending on whether the researchers are looking at students or real workers in organizations.[3] In this chapter, I will focus on real organizational teams wherever possible, but this is not always feasible.

What are the different types of remote teams?

Experts use "virtual," "distributed," "remote," and more recently "hybrid" to describe distinctions in team arrangements that include people working in different locations. However, in practice people tend to use the terms interchangeably; attempts to distinguish between these terms have not really caught on. I will use the term "remote teams" in this chapter.

In this chapter, we will focus on two principal team situations. In the all-remote situation, all team members are located in different places, which could be different buildings (or houses), cities, states, or countries. The part-remote situation has some team members located in one office, with the remaining members scattered in different locations.

Note that I do not distinguish between office and home locations for the team members who are geographically dispersed. This is because post-pandemic, virtual communications are fairly similar in format and quality, whether workers are in an office or in another location. It makes little difference whether a far-flung team member is located in a (far-flung) office or in their own living space. What matters most in a team setting is the location of the team members *relative to each other*.

What are the advantages of remote teams?

While we often hear how difficult it is to work in remote teams, remote teams have significant benefits for the companies that use them. Perhaps the most significant rationale for remote teams is that they provide the opportunity to bring together a broader variety of information, perspectives, and expertise than an organization could find in a single location.[4] Remote teams have become so common that it can be easy to forget how much richness and opportunity they bring to a workplace by expanding the range of potential talent available.

Time zone differences can benefit remote teams, particularly in companies with large and complicated projects. Remote teams spread across time zones can lengthen the effective workday by virtually handing off project work from one time zone to another. For example, a team member in Taipei nearing the end of their day would pass work to a colleague in Frankfurt, who would then pass on the latest version of the work to a colleague in Chicago, and so on. In theory, this allows the company to accomplish tasks much faster because the team has the potential to be effectively operating all the time.

What are the main challenges faced by remote teams?

Beyond the general challenges of virtual communication discussed earlier, the complexity of remote team member locations (and the reliance of team members on each other) introduces additional hurdles. It is difficult to coordinate activities among team members when dispersed workers are unsure about how best to get the information and resources they need from other locations. This is made worse when team members communicate incompletely or ineffectively.[5] The barriers of virtual communication can make collaboration challenging and can inhibit creativity, particularly when it comes to generating new ideas.[6]

Similarly, social dynamics can suffer when team members are not located in the same place. It can take longer or require more effort to develop trust and social cohesion among remote team members.[7] Physical separation can also make it more difficult to understand cultural differences among team members.[8]

As much as time zone differences can prove beneficial to teams, they are also a hindrance when planning meetings, or when team members from different parts of the world need to communicate quickly. Early in my career, when I was still based in the East Coast US-office of a multinational company, a colleague based in Hong Kong said to me that the thirteen-hour time difference between our offices was "simultaneously the best part of the job and the worst part of the job." I learned what he meant when I started working with teams based around the world; in good times, we were able to pass work back and forth, essentially creating a twenty-four-hour workflow. When things were not working as smoothly, it inevitably meant that team members had to stay up late at night to join urgent meetings or risk having important work simply passed around the world, from time zone to time zone. It can certainly be challenging to set up a meeting with a team located in several different time zones. Realistically this can often mean managers expect coworkers to be available in the early mornings or late at night, without extra compensation for working outside of business hours.

The technology that supports remote teamwork has improved dramatically in recent years, but is still a challenge, particularly when one or more team members lose connectivity. If one team member's internet connection fails during a team meeting, this relatively minor event can affect the work of the entire team, and possibly delay key project decisions. Such problems can also lead to frustration from colleagues, even when the error is not due to negligence or errors from the employee.

How do remote teams work together effectively?

Given the complexities listed above, companies should manage all-remote teams somewhat differently from teams in which some of the workers are in the office. Several strategies seem to support remote teamwork effectively.

It is important for the work group to establish a clear team process, which is simply the way that the team agrees to run itself. Establishing a team's process at the beginning of its time together—often through documentation, such as a team charter or team contract—predicts effectiveness for co-located as well as remote teams.[9] Some research suggests that remote teams with well-designed team processes can actually perform *better* than equivalent teams where some members work in the office.[10]

A remote team's process should contain details relevant to the remote setting. A team process typically includes higher-level direction, such as a clear statement of the team's mission and goals, as well as more tactical details, such as the cadence and timing of team meetings.[11] Teams often discuss and agree to methods for decision-making, conflict resolution, and tracking progress at the beginning of the team's work together. Remote team processes should also include guidance on what technology the team will use for different types of communication and information sharing. It is also important to ensure that team members have opportunities to interact with each other informally and get to know each other beyond the scope of the team's task. This can consist of something as simple as a few minutes spent at the beginning of each team meeting discussing what members did over the weekend. Some remote teams structure these conversations; I have worked with global teams in which members shared news or an interesting story about their home country each week, again as a short conversation at the beginning of a team meeting. Such social interaction is important for establishing trust and team cohesion.[12]

Teams often capture their team process in a shared document. These documents are particularly helpful in the early stages of a team's life,[13] and they can also improve performance for teams with less conscientious members.[14] It is important for teams to update and maintain their team process as times change and their work evolves. Perhaps the most important aspect of such documents is the *conversation* that is required to set up and decide upon the team's process. Merely providing employees with a memo outlining procedures is not enough.

It is also important to establish and maintain a climate of "psychological safety." When psychological safety is high in a team, members feel comfortable speaking up, even when admitting to a mistake, asking for help, or dissenting with prevailing team opinion.[15] This sounds simple, but it may be one of the most critical factors supporting team learning.[16] A 2016 *New York Times* article described a two-year research project at Google that sought to predict which groups of people would make high-performing teams. Google ultimately determined that psychological safety was the best predictor, outperforming demographics, social networks, or other personal characteristics.[17] As with team process, psychological safety is a best practice for all teams, but it becomes even more important when team members are remote.[18] Team leaders play a critical role in establishing psychological safety by encouraging team members to speak up and supporting them when they do.[19]

Finally, successful remote teams tend to engage in specific patterns of communication to help overcome the barriers of their physical separation and enhance their efficiency. As with individual virtual work, remote teammates must engage in more deliberate and detailed communication of information, including information about their own situations.[20] Extra communication is also important when new members join an existing team. Newcomers to a remote team are less likely to ask other members about team norms and expectations than they would in a face-to-face setting.[21]

Researchers Chris Riedl and Anita Woolley found that remote teams were more effective when they alternated between periods of relatively intense communication (which they call "bursts") and periods of individual, focused work with little communication. They suggest that remote teams should intentionally plan for patterns of "bursty" communication, rather than having team members send messages and emails in a steady stream at random times.[22] They also note that some teams naturally develop these patterns of communication; I have experienced this more organic communication pattern development in my own remote teamwork, particularly in teams working on innovative projects.

A form of remote teamwork often referred to as "asynchronous work" is becoming more popular among some firms, primarily technology firms with work-from-anywhere policies. This approach to remote teamwork emphasizes written communication that can be answered within a period of time, rather than in a meeting or via chat. In some instances, team members document all their communication in a common repository so that other team members can see it as needed. While synchronous meetings are minimized, teams typically do not eliminate them altogether. Advocates for this approach argue that asynchronous work eliminates much of the pain associated with standard meetings and time zones, and that it provides a better way to document a team's work.[23] While asynchronous work is familiar to some professions (e.g., software development), it is still a relatively new phenomenon, and there is not yet research on its effect on remote teams as a whole.

What style of leadership is best for a remote team?

There is not a single universally effective leadership style. An effective leader is able to correctly diagnose and adapt their style to fit the needs of a given situation.[24] The ideal leadership style for a remote team depends on the nature of the team members, the work that they are doing, and other organizational or environmental factors.

Cornell professor Brad Bell, along with two co-authors, outlined five remote team leadership strategies that have been most supported by empirical research: encouraging self-management, defining the team's mission, establishing expectations and goals, supporting the social climate within the team, and facilitating team members' use of technology.[25] In my own professional experience, a balance between structure and empowerment characterizes many successful remote teams. These strategies are effective for remote teams in part because they allow companies and managers to provide different forms of structure to teams, but do not encourage intensive monitoring or control that workers find oppressive. The team can work effectively in part because its members retain some autonomy.

The factors that predict who *emerges* as a leader in remote teams appear to be somewhat different from those for leadership emergence in traditional office teams. (Leaders "emerge" when there is no designated team leader, and a team member—usually informally—takes on some of the roles of a leader, such as helping to resolve disagreements and providing structure and order to the team's work.[26]) In traditional teams, it is often the most extraverted person, or the one who is most self-confident, who emerges as a leader, regardless of their qualifications. Researchers believe that this happens in part because people often ascribe leadership qualities to those who demonstrate outgoing, confident traits. But people who emerge as leaders in remote teams tend to be more focused on actions, such as the coordination of team members, monitoring of team progress, contribution to team discussion, and support of other team members.[27] This is interesting because it suggests that in traditional teams, the leaders who emerge are often those who talk the most; in remote teams, it may be that leaders are those who do the most work.

How do distributed team members learn to trust each other?

Any relationship requires trust to be sustained and effective over time. And trust is particularly important in a remote setting. A meta-analysis (study of studies) that combined results from more than eighteen hundred teams showed that trust was more tightly linked to performance for remote teams than for face-to-face teams. This is understandable given the additional obstacles to communication and coordination faced by remote teams.[28] One reason for this is that information sharing—a critical success factor for remote teams—increases when there is more trust.[29]

Early studies of virtual communication suggested that teams would struggle to develop trust because people would have less information about each other in a virtual setting.[30] Yet, over time it became clear that remote teams were succeeding in establishing trust and healthy interpersonal relationships, even when members never met in person.[31] Research into this phenomenon in the late 1990s by Sirkka Jarvenpaa and Dorothy Leidner found that these teams were developing a dynamic known as "swift trust"[32] during the initial stages of teamwork to overcome early barriers to normal trust development. Remote teams—and especially team leaders—can help to build swift trust by engaging in at least some social (non-work-related) interaction with teammates, showing initiative-taking and overall enthusiasm.[33]

Swift trust is short-lived and fragile, however. Team members must support it by demonstrating ability, integrity, and benevolence to develop longer-term trust. Remote teams can maintain initial trust levels by establishing a process that allows the team to focus on its task through predictable and timely patterns of communication.[34] Teams can also support longer-term trust by explicitly setting up performance goals and metrics, as well as systems to monitor that performance. Doing so conveys commitment and credibility.[35] It also appears that remote teams can partly address a lack of trust by systematic documentation of their interactions.[36] Regular documentation can compensate for a lack of trust enough to get the team's work done, but it is not enough to build a high-performing, sustainable work group.

How does remoteness affect creativity and innovation in teams?

While researchers have been studying trust on remote teams for decades, there has been less research on creativity and innovation in remote teams.[37] We know that a climate of high psychological safety is important for remote teams working on innovation because it encourages members to speak up with unique ideas and information.[38] Team leaders play a big role in establishing psychological safety but they can also support innovation in remote teams by establishing strong individual relationships and communicating frequently with team members.[39]

It is less clear whether remoteness—physical separation—and virtual communication encourage people to speak up when a team is engaging in creative work. The success of brainstorming in remote teams seems to depend in part on how teams do it. One set of experiments found that brainstorming by remote teams via videoconference produced results of equal quality to efforts by teams meeting in person, while ideas generated by chat (text) communication were worse.[40] But another study found that brainstorming via videoconferencing reduced the number of ideas generated, as compared to in-person meetings, largely because much of the participants' cognitive capacities were spent viewing the meeting video images on their computer screens.[41]

Studies of computer-assisted brainstorming tools have found that participants are more likely to come up with a greater range of ideas than face-to-face teams, but they might struggle more to agree on which idea to pursue. One of the reasons for the greater range of ideas appears to be that these brainstorming tools allow participants to input ideas simultaneously; that is, they do not have to wait for someone else to finish a thought.[42]

What are "subgroup dynamics" in remote teams and how can they affect team performance?

In many teams, subgroups—that is, subsets of team members—become closer with each other, often because of shared similarities. This happens naturally. Younger members go out for drinks after work while older members return home to their families. People on the company softball team develop a connection independent of their duties at work. Subgroups form based on age or on other factors, including gender, ethnic background, job function, or shared hobbies. Team members who have worked together previously, or who were friends prior to the team's initiation, are also prime candidates for subgroup formation. In remote teams, subgroups often form based on the location of members. Teams that have some members based in one location, with other members dispersed in different locations, often find that a subgroup forms among team members based in the same place, often the location of the office itself.

While subgroup formation is a natural social dynamic, it can be damaging to the overall cohesion and performance of the team. The in-office group tends to form a clique with its own set of dynamics and "us-versus-them" mentality about the other team members who are not in their office. Teams with this in-group/out-group configuration are more likely to experience conflict and coordination problems.[43] Sometimes the remote team members form their own clique in reaction to the in-office members joining together.[44] If there are two evenly balanced subgroups, or if subgroups form based on ethnic or national lines, the negative effect on team trust can be even worse.[45]

Interestingly, all-remote teams, in which no one works in the same physical space, exhibit healthier functioning than any configuration of part-remote teams, demonstrating the power of subgroups to damage team performance. For this reason, experts generally recommend that part-remote teams conduct meetings entirely virtually, even if that means that some team members are sitting in offices adjacent to each other on a video call. While this may seem awkward, it helps reduce in-group/out-group dynamics by making all team members equal during formal meetings.

6

COMPANIES: OPTIMIZING VIRTUAL AND REMOTE WORK PRACTICES

In this chapter, we will focus on the issues that companies face related to remote and hybrid work, rather than individuals, managers, or teams. Of course, companies are also made up of individuals, managers, and teams, but the issues that we address in this chapter are typically the domain of a few senior leaders, rather than dozens or hundreds of mid-level leaders. When I refer to companies taking some sort of action in this chapter, I am generally referring to this senior leadership team.

What are the benefits of remote work to employers?

Working from home can result in increased productivity for many employees, and working from anywhere can yield even greater productivity gains. In some types of businesses, especially in firms with many workers doing relatively independent work (think software engineers or customer service agents), increased productivity can be a major benefit of remote work. Productivity increases flow directly to company profits, as employees are producing more without a concurrent increase in labor cost.

Remote work has also become an important tool for employee recruitment and retention, particularly for jobs requiring scarce expertise. A survey run by compensation consultancy Payscale in late 2022 reported that 55 percent of employers believed that remote work was affecting the way they competed for talent, up from 47 percent one year prior. The proportion reporting this impact was even higher for larger firms.

Some employers have also begun to use remote work as a trade-off to higher wages. Even before the pandemic people were, on average, willing to take an 8 percent pay cut in order to work remotely.[1] Post-pandemic surveys continue to report significant proportions of the working population willing to accept a pay cut in order to continue working at home at least part of the time.[2] Several economists reported in 2022 that many employers used remote work to keep pay increases for remote workers lower than they would have been otherwise.[3]

Companies with remote workers can also increase profits by reducing their office space, but this typically requires changing office configurations. In recent years, many companies running in a hybrid-work model have reduced real estate costs by requiring employees to share office spaces, either in assigned pairs or by having employees reserve desk space in advance (a practice known as "hoteling").[4]

How does office hoteling work, and how is it different from "hot desking"?

Hoteling and hot desking both refer to office arrangements in which employees use shared workspaces (that is, they do not have dedicated desks or offices). The terms are often used interchangeably, but they are somewhat different. Hot desking is an unstructured arrangement in which employees find an available desk when they come into the office (and may risk not finding a desk on days in which the office is busy). Hoteling allows employees to reserve a desk in advance of coming into the office, similar to reserving a hotel room. Well before the pandemic, hoteling was already a growing trend, especially among firms with many employees who traveled or worked remotely.[5]

Many advances in hoteling models originate from professional services firms. In a 2018 interview, Kevin Virostek, the CEO of the consultancy EY, described the firm's newly opened, 100 percent hoteling office in Tysons Corner, Virginia, noting, "There are not prominent executive offices . . . today, I am sitting in a workstation with an executive assistant on one side and a new staff member on the other . . . being in that proximity allows me to mentor as needed. However, when I need space to conduct a confidential conversation or meeting, I can utilize one of our private rooms."

Virostek also described how technology can enable hoteling to go beyond just booking a space to work: "When I arrive at the office in the morning, I can pull up a 3D image of the space and can see where everyone I need to work with that day is sitting . . . once I am checked in, my technology follows me, and my phone number connects to my selected location."[6] Since the time of this interview, hoteling technology has also added features allowing employers to track office density data, and alert managers if a space is becoming too crowded.[7]

While companies use both practices, researchers generally consider hoteling preferable; the unstructured nature of hot desking can cause employees to waste time looking for a desk. Hot desking has also been linked to reduced trust and morale among employees.[8]

Why are some employers resistant to remote work?

There are essentially three reasons that employers cite when criticizing remote or hybrid work as being bad for business.[9] Two of these reasons link to concerns about reduced productivity, and the third reflects concerns about diminished creativity and collaboration.

The first point of resistance is the "slacking" argument, or the belief that employees will not work as hard when they are not in the office. And, in the period immediately following the pandemic lockdowns, popular media was rife with anecdotal accounts of "ghosting, coasting, slacking, and cyberloafing," as described in a 2022 *Fortune* article.[10] Career coach Bryan Creely coined the term "quiet quitting" in a TikTok post in early 2022 to describe working the bare minimum to stay employed. By the end of the year, this term was considered a significant workplace trend.[11]

A 2022 Microsoft survey of hybrid workers showed that, while 87 percent of employees surveyed reported that they were productive, 85 percent of leaders said that "the shift to hybrid work has made it challenging to have confidence that employees are being productive," a paradox that Microsoft calls "productivity paranoia."[12] Microsoft notes that metrics from its Office 365 software (which includes the Teams application) suggest that employees are probably more accurate in their assessment of productivity.

While there have been ebbs and flows in productivity in the US economy as a whole since 2005 (when researchers first began to track it), there is no empirical data to link productivity declines to remote or hybrid work. At the same time, working from home, or working from anywhere, can lead to significant increases in worker output, at least for certain types of jobs.[13] And, it is important to note that there have always been slackers at work; most of us can think of co-workers who spent hours looking busy while surfing the internet or texting with friends and family. Overall, there is not reliable evidence that remote or hybrid situations have led more employees to neglect their work.

So, how do we reconcile the productivity doubts expressed by company leaders with the evidence that, if anything, productivity increases in a remote work environment? The two remaining employer concerns partly (but not entirely) explain why leaders feel the way they do.

Company leaders are correct that remote work can make communication and coordination, as well as collaboration and creativity, more challenging. It takes additional effort to ensure that everyone in a work group has correct information or that team members are coordinating their efforts when co-workers are not in the same place. Similarly, when there is no way to drop by someone's office quickly, it is not as easy to ask a question or share a sudden idea. It is easier to talk to someone than it is to email or even message them. Yet, these challenges are not new; they existed long before remote work became widespread. For decades, multinational companies have been developing practices to address all these challenges in both globally distributed teams and in offshored or outsourced operations.[14]

Some experts believe that employers' resistance to remote and hybrid work is due in part to the way that leaders approach the transition to remote and hybrid work. Many employers fail to grasp how much they need to transform to meet the demands of today's business environment. In an interview with the *Boston Globe*, Harvard Business School professor Tsedal Neeley described employer concerns about remote and hybrid work as "a leadership failure," noting, "most employers are almost in denial that work has changed forever."[15] Companies often try to superimpose traditional in-office policies and traditions on remote or hybrid work schedules, and do not give sufficient attention to the significant change in day-to-day operations brought about by this shift.

How do companies decide on the number of work-from-home days to offer employees?

We have previously discussed how the true optimal amount of remote work varies by individual, depending on the nature of their work and their own preferences and characteristics. But most hybrid-work companies prefer to set broad guidelines for their employees, and so must consider higher-level factors.

Certainly, the preferences of both workers and managers factor into company decision-making. It appears that employees on average prefer to work from home about three days per week.[16] Managers' preferences for the amount that their employees work remotely have been shifting since the beginning of the pandemic, but generally fall a bit lower, around two days per week.[17] Unsurprisingly, company policies tend to follow managers' preferences.[18]

When setting work-from-home levels, company leaders also consider the nature of the work and may vary remote work allowances across different departments. For example, companies generally allow—or even require—software engineers to work entirely remotely, given that their jobs demand a lot of focused work and most of their collaboration with others normally takes place online. Company leaders should consider many factors to determine the optimal split between in-office and home-based work for a given company, including the type of work performed by employees, typical commute time, and even national culture.

How does requiring (rather than allowing) remote work affect worker motivation and job satisfaction?

Allowing people to work remotely typically increases motivation because it increases their autonomy, or their ability to determine on their own how they will do their work.[19]

It can also be motivating for those who had wanted to work remotely (or already were doing so) when a company *mandates* remote work for employees. But for those who preferred working in the office, the forced shift to working from home can result in a loss of motivation.

Most research on the effects of mandatory remote work was completed during the first two years of the COVID-19 pandemic. Given all the other factors in play then, it is no surprise that this research links mandatory remote work and reduced productivity and performance.[20] However, this research probably does not reflect a post-pandemic reality because most of its data was collected during times when children were out of school, there was heightened uncertainty and stress, and normal services (e.g., housecleaners, daycare, and restaurants) were often unavailable.

There is, however, some pre-pandemic research that indirectly supports the notion that not giving employees a choice as to whether or not they work remotely could be enough to have negative effects on employees. In one 2013 study set in Singapore, researchers found that employees who were given the option to work remotely *but chose not to do so* reported similar work–life balance and perceived similar work–life balance support as their colleagues who had chosen to work remotely.[21] At the same time, employees whose requests for remote work had been denied reported much lower levels of support than even employees whose jobs made remote infeasible.[22] These results suggest that having a choice over work conditions could make a difference.

Finally, because companies often put in place required remote work to reduce office space, even employees who want to work remotely often find that their newfound location flexibility comes with the loss of their dedicated workspace in the office, as employers move to hoteling practices. I have spoken to managers who are at once avid advocates of remote work *and* insistent that they have their own office space available on the one or two days that they come into the office each week. I understand the sentiment behind these positions, but I generally encourage such managers to consider the business implications of holding dedicated real estate that will be used less than 50 percent of the time.

What is a remote work policy and what does it include?

A survey run by human resources consultancy Mercer in late 2022 found that, more than two years after the COVID-19 pandemic began, only 34 percent of employers with remote workers reported having a formal set of rules guiding their employees' remote work practices, while 48 percent relied on informal guidelines and 17 percent took a "hands-off approach."[23] This statistic is somewhat surprising given that well-developed remote or hybrid work policies can help ensure equity among employees, protect company information, and help the company avoid any related legal liability.

Laurel Farrer, founder and president of the Remote Work Association, notes that a formal remote work policy typically includes guidelines for employee contracts, occupational health and safety, and information security, in addition to any measures needed to ensure compliance with immigration laws, employment and labor laws, and tax regulations.[24]

Remote work policies typically also set overall standards for determining who is eligible for remote work, amounts of remote work allowed or required, and a process for performance evaluation and possible reversal of remote work privileges in the case of poor performance. Ideally, these standards at a corporate level ensure equity among employees, but also leave some flexibility for different business units and functional areas to determine work-appropriate allowances.

Equity among workers is an important reason for these policies. A 2022 *BBC* news article profiled one Ohio-based software engineer whose five-person team was required to return to the office full-time, even though they had been working effectively in a remote setting and despite the fact that senior leaders continued to work all-remotely, some traveling as digital nomads. "We've had company-wide meetings where these employees were videoing in from vacation spots," noted the employee. "Someone must have pointed out the optics—they've had their cameras off in the last few meetings."[25] Indeed, perceptions of inequity among different groups of can lead to resentment and cliques of in-office and out-of-office employees,[26] all of which is typically damaging to organizational performance.[27]

Do companies pay work-from-anywhere employees based on the company location or on the employee's location?

Historically, remote workers live within commuting distance of their office. However, as the work-from-anywhere trend has taken off, it is more common to see workers moving to locations that may be cheaper than their employer's location. During the pandemic, many employees based in expensive metro areas like San Francisco or New York discovered that they could enjoy a much greater quality of life (and have a much larger home-office space) in lower-cost locations far removed from their employer.[28]

As some employers began to announce longer-term remote work policies in mid-2020, they took varying approaches to dealing with the differential in an employee's pay and their actual cost of living. In May 2020, Facebook was the first large employer to announce plans to adjust all-remote employees' pay to match the cost of living in their residential locations.[29] By mid-2021, most other large technology firms based in Silicon Valley had followed suit.[30] Other companies, such as Zillow, opted to pay the same salary, regardless of location. Some companies have taken a more nuanced approach, basing pay on a single city in each country, or focusing on regional differentials.[31]

It is possible that in another few years, the debate about the location basis of pay will have resolved into industry or even national standards. Some experts believe that for some types of jobs with high levels of remote work, a national market rate for labor will eventually emerge, reflecting national demand and supply, and adjusted for individual employees' capabilities and experiences.[32] For some jobs that are nearly always all-remote, such as software engineers, this national convergence may have already occurred. Outside of the technology field, however, there is not yet a standard set of practices.

What technologies are companies investing in to facilitate effective virtual and remote work?

As remote work becomes prevalent and more permanent, companies are increasingly investing in collaboration software to handle logistics related to remote workers, hybrid offices, and cloud-based technologies. A 2022 survey of IT professionals by technology media firm Foundry found that 54 percent of responding firms were investing in enhanced collaboration and meeting tools, while 31 percent were investing in employee hoteling applications and 19 percent in meeting room reservation systems.[33] IT consultancy Gartner forecasted corporate investment in cloud technologies to grow 22 percent in 2022, compared to a 3 percent overall growth in IT spending.[34]

Collaboration software is actually a category that includes functionality ranging from videoconferencing and text messaging to real-time online whiteboarding, work-flow tracking, and document sharing. Some companies combine multiple software applications to build a suite of collaboration software, while others invest in an integrated solution—Microsoft Teams is one common example of the latter.[35] Both approaches have their advantages, and company leaders typically evaluate the specific needs of their employees and project teams as part of deciding on an approach.[36]

Previously in this chapter, we touched on the practices of hoteling and hot desking that are becoming more popular, as more companies move to a hybrid model of work. Unless desk-sharing is set out on a fixed schedule in advance, technology is needed to manage reservations of desks and other office resources shared among hoteling employees, and to allow employees to plan their work locations and find co-workers.[37] Additionally, as in-office time is increasingly used for team meetings and other collaborative work, companies are finding that they need scheduling software for their meeting rooms.

Many companies have increased or accelerated their investment in cloud-based technologies in response to increased remote work.[38] Cloud-based storage allows companies to store data on secure servers with encryption and backup measures, as opposed to local servers in company offices or (worse yet) individual employees' computer hard drives. A company that bases its work applications and software in the cloud can make updates and fix problems more quickly and can push changes out to individual employees in a centralized way, rather than having to install updates on each individual computer. To handle the security risks of transferring confidential information between the cloud and individual remote users, many companies have also increased their identity and access management capability, with features such as two-factor authentication previously found in only a fraction of firms.[39]

How are companies monitoring remote workers?

There are many ways that employers can legally monitor employees, whether they actually do so or not. Employers can read anything sent by or received from an employee's work email address, and they can usually see what internet websites employees are visiting. Monitoring software can collect data from workers, including the websites they access and the amount of time they spend in different software applications, and can take randomly timed screenshots of employees' current screens, among other functions. Companies can also use relatively inexpensive technology to track drivers or other employees using company vehicles.[40]

While different types of electronic performance monitoring technology have been in place for a long time in production-related jobs, such as manufacturing and fast food restaurants, the use of monitoring of white-collar and professional employees' activities was relatively minor until the pandemic. But monitoring software became much more interesting to many employers when employees were sent home during COVID-19 shutdowns. One widely cited survey reported a nearly 1,700 percent increase in internet searches on the term "how to monitor employees working from home" in March 2020, compared to a year prior.[41]

Research on the effects of electronic performance monitoring taken as a whole shows relatively small—although all negative—effects on employees' job satisfaction (lower), stress (higher), and counterproductive behaviors at work (higher).[42] The true effects become clearer, however, when the different uses of monitoring are considered individually. The purpose of monitoring makes a big difference. Monitoring that is used to help employees do better (but not used to punish employees) is generally viewed positively, and it can result in greater productivity. For example, a retailer could monitor a customer service agent's calls or text chats to help them improve their relationship-building, service level, and even their efficiency.[43] However, monitoring that is used primarily to surveil and punish is linked to outcomes such as decreased job satisfaction and increased stress. The same retailer might choose to monitor the agent's call times to surveil their overall productivity; this practice would more likely be demotivating to the agent.[44] Even worse is monitoring that is used to gather employee data with no apparent purpose; this "authoritarian" monitoring strategy can lead to increased counterproductive employee behaviors.[45]

Even with more benign performance monitoring, research often finds that employees can end up paying too much attention to the metrics being monitored at the expense of their actual job tasks.[46] Monitoring can also lead workers to spend time trying to "beat" the monitoring systems, with one study showing monitored employees more likely to cheat than unmonitored employees.[47]

I typically recommend against most types of employee performance monitoring, other than the type that is used to help the employee, with real-time feedback and praise when warranted, not with punishment. I often suggest to company leaders that they should aim for the type of monitoring that many people enjoy on their smartwatches—the kind that can nudge us along to developing good habits and behaviors—I sometimes call this the "Fitbit versus Big Brother" approach to monitoring.

How do companies handle large-scale layoffs when many remote workers are involved?

One of the most disturbing trends to emerge in recent years is the increasing number of employers conducting mass layoffs of remote employees by short text messages or emails, or even simply disconnecting employees' access to the employers' information systems. A similar action was roundly criticized in 2006, when retailer Radio Shack laid off four hundred (mostly in-office) employees by email.[48] In 2023, some twelve thousand employees laid off by Google reported that they learned they were fired when the company cut them off from their email access.[49] According to reports from former employees, other, mainly technology, companies such as Amazon, Meta, and Twitter have taken similar actions in large-scale layoffs of both in-office and remote employees.[50]

While some have speculated that these layoffs took place by email due to tight staffing in human resources departments,[51] it is likely that remoteness also played a role. The decision to lay off people by email becomes easier if company leaders do not have to see those people around the office.

It turns out that this type of action is not just cruel, but it is also bad for business. There is longstanding research showing that treating laid-off employees with dignity and respect supports the motivation of remaining employees. Disrespectful treatment can increase retaliatory actions by remaining employees, many of whom also face increased workloads following layoffs.[52] It is possible that some of these employers will come to regret their actions if remaining employees become less motivated and begin to look for new jobs. However, it is also possible that the market strength of these large employers will be enough to make email and text-based layoffs a new reality, and essentially a trade-off that employees make for the opportunity to work remotely.

7

GOVERNMENT AND SOCIETY: THE IMPACT OF WIDESPREAD REMOTE WORK

Even before 2020, people promoted the idea of remote work to try to improve society. Scientist Jack Nilles encouraged working from home using technology with the hope that it could reduce the environmental impact of commuting.[1] As early as the late 1990s, as internet availability and bandwidth increased, a few countries were already contending with influxes of work-from-anywhere "digital nomads."[2] Some enterprising local governments began developing policies to attract remote workers.[3] The US federal government had long been relatively flexible about hybrid and remote work before 2020.

Because of these early experiences, some governments were more prepared than others for the explosion of remote work arrangements that began with the COVID-19 pandemic. Yet our understanding of the overall societal impact of widespread remote work is still incomplete. In this chapter, we will review what is known and consider the questions not yet answered.

Does remote work help or hurt the environment?

The environmental impact of working from home is one of the most important open questions of interest to governments and society. It seems logical that avoiding a commute and not requiring an office would reduce emissions. And yet, working from home creates additional environmental burdens. Researchers have been working to determine whether the environmental savings outweigh the new costs, but the impact of hybrid work complicates these analyses. London Business School's Ioannis Ioannou, a longtime expert in corporate sustainability, notes, "There is indeed no consensus that working from home is better for the environment . . . I would be surprised if any company would claim this as an environmental improvement."[4]

It is tempting to cite the reduced CO_2 and other greenhouse gas emissions of the early pandemic months as evidence of the environmental benefits of remote work.[5] Yet data from this era—even that collected in urban areas—is flawed because it represents a world in which work in many manufacturing and service businesses shut down entirely. By the end of 2021, even as remote work continued at relatively high levels, worldwide CO_2 and other greenhouse gas emissions rebounded to set a new record, with all sectors except for transportation and household usage returning to or exceeding pre-pandemic levels.[6] Even the transportation and household sectors' usage met or slightly exceeded early 2019 levels, suggesting that there was little lasting benefit gained from massive migration out of offices. The United States exhibited similar trends, with January to April 2022 energy consumption slightly higher than the same period in 2019, and higher levels in the residential, commercial, and manufacturing sectors more than offsetting a modest reduction in the transportation sector.[7]

Savings that come from remote work can vary dramatically. A hybrid-working company that allows its employees to retain their dedicated workspaces at the office and has at least some employees coming to the office every day will realize less savings than, say, a company that reduces its overall office space and organizes employees to come to the office on assigned days using shared workspaces.

Even as offices save on energy costs, employees working from home are still consuming energy, just at a different location and in different ways. Employees working in hybrid situations often need two sets of computing equipment (or at least peripherals), as well as office furniture and additional computing bandwidth from their home offices. The manufacture and maintenance of this equipment alone is a significant source of energy usage.[8]

New types of travel are another consequence of remote work. Because of the increased work flexibility enjoyed by many remote workers, and (in some cases) the availability of an additional automobile at the house during weekdays, remote workers and their family members sometimes drive *more* than they did when they worked in offices full time. Another potential source of additional travel comes from the segment of the population that moved to locations further away from their offices after starting remote work.[9] For those who continue to commute at least some days to the office, their commute distances are now longer and consume more energy. Additionally, their new suburban or ex-urban houses are often larger than before and consume more energy.[10]

In 2020, one group of researchers summarized the results of thirty-nine (pre-pandemic) empirical studies of the environmental impact of remote work.[11] They found that of the thirty-nine papers, twenty-six showed that remote working decreased net energy use, while eight papers demonstrated the opposite. However, the analyses in the papers used different assumptions and considered different variables. The authors found that some papers considered relatively few costs of remote work, which could result in an overestimation of environmental savings. The researchers conclude that, while remote work more likely has a positive overall impact on the environment, the extent could be modest.

Beyond the costs and benefits of not commuting, other variables affect the extent to which remote work influences the environment. Many of these variables—such as climate; type of energy used for home heating and cooling; and average sizes of homes, cars, and offices—differ across populations. Even if scientists accurately analyze the impact on one population, it is unlikely to apply to other populations.

A 2019 analysis from the engineering firm WSP provides a good example of the risks inherent in generalizing environmental impact analyses. The analysis used the case of a prototypical UK worker in a two-hundred-person office to argue that, while working from home could reduce greenhouse gases for the worker in the summer, it could increase emissions in the winter.[12] The researchers recommended that companies consider seasonal remote work, with employees working from home in the summer and from the office in the winter.

This recommendation could be useful (albeit difficult to implement) for a firm located in the UK, where it is common for houses to not have air conditioning, while most larger offices do. Furthermore, a majority of UK homes rely on CO_2-producing fossil fuels for heat in the winter.[13] Because of this, it makes sense to think that people could reduce their environmental impact by saving on both home heating in the winter and office air conditioning in the summer.

Policymakers should consider the nuances of climate and energy usage in different areas of the world. It would be a mistake to generalize the conclusions of the WSP analysis beyond remarkably similar populations.[14] For example, in the United States, 66 percent of all homes use energy-intensive central air conditioning to cool their homes in the summer, with greater concentrations in the southern states.[15] In the southern US it would, therefore, benefit the environment more to encourage the opposite policy and have employees work from home in the winter and go to offices in the summer.

There is one benefit that looks to last beyond the pandemic. Concentrated pollution in urban areas, especially during traditional rush hours, has somewhat alleviated because fewer people are moving in and out of the city center every day.[16] In addition to the environmental benefits that come from reduced commuting, this dispersion also leads to reduced traffic congestion and demands on both roads and public transit. This shift could improve the quality of life even for those who still must commute. The balancing of geographic dispersion of people during the workday may end up being the most significant environmental (and societal) gain of the pandemic.

What are some other societal benefits and costs of remote work?

Before we become too sanguine about the benefits of a lower concentration of workers in cities, we must also consider the losses suffered in these urban areas, including shuttered restaurants and shops. One UK study of spending on "local personal services," such as restaurant meals, coffees, gym memberships, and haircuts, found an average 7 percent decrease in such spending in neighborhoods, to which there was a 20 percent decrease in overall commuting.[17] Within that average, however, were concerning spikes: a summary of the study noted that one central London neighborhood was expected to lose around eight thousand jobs related to personal spending declines, a number that nearly matched the neighborhood's residential population of 9,271. Yet, the researchers involved in the study expected companies to create a similar number of jobs within the

161 neighborhoods experiencing the greatest increases in personal service spending—with a total population of more than 1.5 million.

Society sees a similar trade-off in smaller cities and towns with traditionally fewer employment opportunities. There have been some economic benefits for these areas, as residents enjoy a greater range of available jobs that no longer require them to move out of the area. Similarly, the migration of some remote employees out of urban areas has brought new spending and economic activity into areas that previously struggled. Despite these benefits, in some areas the higher wages earned by some newly arrived work-from-anywhere workers combined with increased demand for housing have resulted in what some call remote work gentrification, where higher real estate costs hurt or even displace the original residents of these communities.[18]

Some of the most extreme examples of this displacement in the United States come from the Central Mountain states, due to their relative proximity to the technology hubs of San Francisco and Seattle. Workers in those two metro areas, feeling the pinch of high housing costs, learned that they could both afford more and enjoy a higher-quality life characterized by cleaner air, lower crime rates, and easier access to nature by moving to smaller cities in Utah, Idaho, or Montana. As a result, housing costs in locations such as Boise, Idaho, and Bozeman, Montana, increased by about 50 percent between 2019 and 2021, a trend that is not expected to reverse.[19]

Housing costs in Mexico City have increased similarly since the beginning of the pandemic, with landlords converting desirable real estate into short-term rentals at much higher prices to accommodate an influx of remote workers.[20] However, many countries in Europe— with rapidly aging rural populations and younger urban populations—view remote work as a way to encourage re-population and revitalization of rural communities.[21]

Migration aside, an enduring advantage of remote work is that it creates a greater talent pool for employers, and it enables people to join the workforce who might not otherwise be able to do so. The Society for Human Resource Management reported that employers who move to remote work find a much larger pool of candidates to hire.[22] Some of the additional applicants come from different locations, but others are people with disabilities who would not have been able to work in an office setting.

How is remote work legally regulated by governments in different countries?

In the Netherlands, a 2022 law gave employees the right to request remote work from their employers and limits the reasons companies can use to justify refusing the requests.[23] This legislation has been described by some as the first national labor law establishing an employee's right to work remotely.[24] Many other countries established permanent legislation or regulations related to remote work in recent years. In early 2023, global insurer and consultancy Lockton found twenty-three countries on five continents had implemented permanent remote work legislation.[25]

Notably absent from this list is the United States. The developed country with the fewest labor regulations, the US federal government has not addressed remote work as a regulatory issue. As with other employment conditions, such as paid vacation time and severance pay, US employers are not subject to any national regulations related to remote work other than taxes and immigration requirements for cross-border workers. This employer freedom stands in contrast to other countries, in which governments—as well as labor unions—take an active role in crafting regulation of remote work with different policy aims in different countries.

For example, Italy has a complex regulatory framework covering remote work that requires companies to come to an agreement with employees (often through union negotiations) on a remote work labor regime. Companies can employ remote workers under a teleworking arrangement in which companies can hire people to work from a fixed location, on a fixed schedule. Or, in a newer arrangement chosen by many employers, employees can follow a "smart working" regime, in which they can work from any location and are evaluated based on the achievement of objectives, rather than the completion of specific work hours.[26]

Another set of labor laws in some (mainly European) countries prohibits managers from contacting employees outside of established working hours.[27] These "right to disconnect" laws apply to all workers, and many were already in place years before the uptick in remote work. But they provide particular support to remote workers, who often have a tougher time separating work from home life.

Within the United States, are there any state labor laws that affect remote workers?

In the United States there are a variety of state-level labor laws that can be challenging to navigate. An employer with remote employees in other states must, in many cases, immediately implement the labor laws of that state. The variety and diversity of state regulations mean companies can become liable for failing to comply with state programs or mandates, including paid leave requirements or minimum wage laws, which vary considerably by state.[28]

There may also be legal obligations for employers who wish to make remote work mandatory, particularly if those employees were originally hired as in-office workers. The employer must first seek advice to determine if forcing in-office workers to switch to working from home is legal in their jurisdiction, and under their existing employment contracts with employees.[29] In many cases, employers can make this switch, but they may be required by law to provide employees a stipend for office furniture and other tools with which to do their jobs in their home workspace.[30]

How do different tax laws between US states affect remote workers and their employers?

The taxation of both workers and their employers also varies by state, and by the specific pairing of employee and company states. Some states that have had cross-border commuting for decades (such as New Jersey and Pennsylvania) already have in place reciprocity or "reverse credit" agreements that protect employers and employees from double taxation.[31] In other states, double taxation is a real possibility.

For employers, this problem arises due to "physical presence" tax laws originally meant to ensure that employers with offices in a given state were (via corporate taxes) paying for public services that they were using in the state. However, in some states, these laws require an employer to register in the state and to pay related business and employment taxes, even if they have only one employee working in that state.

For employees, double taxation is a risk in fewer locations, but there are still several states that tax employees based on the location of the company, rather than the location of the employee. If an employee works for an employer in one of those "convenience of the employer" states, they must pay income tax to that state, even if they live somewhere else. If their state of residence levies state income tax based on employee location, the employee has to file state tax returns in both states and may owe taxes to both.[32]

How do work-from-anywhere employees manage to live and work outside of their home country?

It's important to differentiate between a standard remote worker, who works at a specific location other than the employer's, and digital nomads, who repeatedly move from location to location while working for a single employer. This can be an important distinction regarding country tax laws because many countries have special short-term visas and tax plans for digital nomads who expect to be in the country for a relatively short period.

As of late 2022, dozens of countries offer various versions of visas targeting remote workers.[33] These visas allow their holders to live in one country and work for a company located elsewhere.[34] In most cases, visa holders pay taxes to their home country (where their employer is located), and not in the country where they are living temporarily. Digital nomad visas are frequently time-limited, typically ranging from three to twelve months. These visas differ from traditional work visas in that the digital nomad visa-holder cannot accept work with a local employer, and they typically must prove that they are drawing a minimum salary from their home-country employer.

One concern raised by tax experts is that increasing numbers of digital nomads (who tend to be highly educated and well-paid) will seek out low-tax jurisdictions to live and work, and they will continue to move among those jurisdictions. The net impact of this migration pattern could be a drain of tax revenues in these workers' home countries.[35]

For longer-term work-from-anywhere employees, cross-border legal challenges can be more daunting. Living long-term in a country different from a worker's employer often requires registering as a "tax resident," and paying taxes to the country of residence. In some cases, immigration hurdles increase as the employee's stay becomes more permanent; employees often must establish themselves as independent contractors or another similar status. In this situation, double taxation becomes a greater risk.[36] Some countries (particularly in the European Union) are establishing cross-border tax agreements for remote workers, and the OECD has pledged to further promote this trend of tax simplification.[37] But full tax reform for remote workers is still years away.

What are regional and local governments doing to attract remote workers?

Countries can recruit digital nomads and other remote workers through special visas and tax reforms. But recruiting remote workers also occurs *within* countries, as different (usually smaller) cities and regions compete to attract work-from-anywhere employees. The two most common tactics used by these communities are investment in technology and other amenities, and direct incentive payments for workers who move to the community.

The increased dispersion of remote workers during the workweek means that spending patterns have shifted. Many people who used to spend money on lunches or gym memberships near their workplaces are now getting these things closer to home. They are still buying the same things; they are just buying them in different places. But this move to remote work creates a demand for services that used to be available near the office.

Analysis from Harvard University's Joint Center for Housing Studies suggests that neighborhood amenities, such as restaurants and other shops, and access to

high-speed internet, will become more important for remote workers.[38] This reprioritization means that some
appealing urban areas could continue to experience high
demand for housing, while other urban neighborhoods
could experience an outflow of residents. Suburban
neighborhoods without this type of localized commercial and technological infrastructure may become less appealing. Another report, from the Pew Charitable Trusts,
notes that the increase in remote work could lead cities
and states to emphasize shared workspaces, broadband
availability, and more competitive tax rates over traditional city features like commuter transit and dense
housing.[39]

In North Dakota, Commissioner of Commerce James
Lieman claimed that, in addition to providing high-speed
internet, now "communities across the state are revitalizing
their downtowns so you're seeing new amenities, updated
attractions, more walkable neighborhoods."[40] In Minnesota,
the state's Department of Employment and Economic
Development began in 2014 to make a series of targeted
investments in high-speed broadband internet in a number
of its smaller towns and cities. This initiative developed
into a program called "Telecommuter Forward!" which,
as of August 2022, had certified forty-seven communities
supporting and promoting telecommuting.[41]

Some governments have turned to direct cash incentives
to lure remote workers to move to their communities. One
of the oldest of these programs is Oklahoma's Tulsa Remote
initiative. The program, founded in 2018, promises a pay-
ment of $10,000 to qualified remote workers who move to
Tulsa for at least a year. The program goes beyond the cash
incentive to include activities and services that help new
arrivals integrate into the community.[42] Two different impact analyses of the program reported positive net results
for both the city[43] and the workers who participated in the

program.[44] Similar incentive programs thrive in Vermont, Georgia, and Kansas.[45]

Outside of the United States, other countries are starting to offer incentives to their younger citizens to move to rural areas with slower economies and aging populations. The World Economic Forum lists rural relocation programs in countries including Portugal, Ireland, and Italy.[46] Typical incentive payments for these programs cover most or all of a modest rental for one year and also require at least one year of residency.

Many newer programs offer both money and other perks. Yet, questions remain about the overall demand for these incentives and the willingness of remote workers to move. A *Harvard Business Review* article emphasized the importance of community involvement in the design and development of this type of program, to both increase community acceptance of the new (often relatively highly paid) residents, and to identify ways to integrate the newcomers into the local community. Research on Tulsa Remote's success suggests that while the economic incentives may induce people to move somewhere new, successful integration with the community is what convinces them to remain beyond the required minimum period.[47]

8

FUTURE TRENDS IN REMOTE AND VIRTUAL WORK

Speculating about the future is risky. This sort of thing is particularly challenging with a topic as dynamic and rapidly evolving as remote work. But thinking about the future here is worthwhile because it can help us understand general trends and make better decisions today. The future of remote work will affect companies' investments in technology and their organizational structures. Changes in offices and work environments will also have dramatic consequences for individual workers' career trajectories.

Could we see a significant reduction in remote work from current levels?

According to the monthly US Survey of Working Arrangements and Attitudes, by the end of 2022 the average American worker did 30 percent of their work at home. Some 68 percent of the workers who could work remotely did so at least part of each week.[1] These statistics have been stable for a year, suggesting that the amount of remote work in the United States has hit an equilibrium. Stanford economist Nick Bloom, one of the authors of the survey, noted in an interview that "We are all back to pre-pandemic trends in online shopping, but permanently up on online work."[2]

The initial post-pandemic years brought labor shortages to many sectors of the US economy, including those where people could work remotely. As a result, employees enjoyed more power to negotiate their work conditions, just as employers were trying to bring their employees back to the office. In many cases, employees prevailed and companies, to recruit and retain talented people, had to be more flexible about remote work.

We can see this power of workers in the labor market by comparing employer plans and employee preferences for remote work from 2020 to 2022. While employee preferences for remote work stayed about the same over the period (at just under three days per week), employers had to become more comfortable with remote work; their policies for remote work increased by 44 percent, from 1.6 days of at-home working in mid-2020 to 2.3 days per week in late 2022.[3]

The relative power of workers in the labor market ebbs and flows with the economy and a wave of layoffs that began in early 2023 may be a sign of changes to come.[4] If more people want jobs, companies will—at least in theory—have more power to cut down on how much remote work they allow, either by listing new job openings as in-office or by reducing the allowed amount of remote work for existing employees (who will be less likely to leave).

Yet many experts believe companies aren't going to force a massive return to physical offices anytime soon, for two reasons. First, remote work is a powerful tool for recruiting and retaining talent. While higher unemployment would give companies more leverage in hiring, they are still likely to lose their *most talented* people, who can find new (remote) jobs even in a tough hiring market.[5] Second, forcing people into physical offices—particularly during a business slowdown—increases company operating costs at a time when employers are looking to cut costs. Furthermore, many employers have already eliminated office space and have enjoyed spending less on real estate and utilities.

Will remote work become more common in the future?

As much as a significant reduction in remote work seems unlikely, there is also a low probability of a significant increase. The current plateau in rates of remote work is the product of two years during which employers and workers effectively negotiated allowable amounts of remote work as companies returned from pandemic lockdowns. During this period, there was certainly an opportunity for remote work to remain at higher levels, but it decreased. The apparent stability at current levels suggests that, with our currently available technology (and barring another crisis at the level of COVID-19), we are unlikely to see higher levels of remote work anytime soon.

Why the caveat of "with currently available technology"? Just as the digitization of information and graphics of the past forty years enabled today's model of remote work, further advances in technology over coming decades will likely shape a different model of work, which may include more remote work. Emerging tools that show some promise for remote work include immersive technologies, such as virtual reality, augmented reality, and the metaverse, as well as artificial intelligence–based tools that are focusing on improving virtual meetings and communications.

What technological changes could really increase the rate of remote work?

Remote work depends crucially on the now familiar use of videoconferencing and collaborative workspaces, but more may be coming. "Immersive technologies" and the "metaverse," while perhaps overhyped, have very real potential to really change how we work in the future.

First, some brief definitions. "Immersive technologies" are a category of technologies that merge elements of the physical world with digital content. The two most common types of immersive technologies are "virtual reality" and "augmented reality." Virtual reality (VR) puts the user into a digitally created virtual environment and allows the user to manipulate parts of that environment. Within the environment, a digital figure called an "avatar" typically represents the user. Some VR experiences require special headsets and other equipment (e.g., gloves or handheld controllers)—these tend to be more immersive, giving users the sense of existing in the virtual world. Other VR experiences occur entirely on a computer screen, with users moving within the virtual world by using mouse clicks and keystrokes.

Augmented reality (AR) technology differs from VR in that it overlays digital images onto real-world images, thus "augmenting" physical reality rather than creating a completely different reality. One example of the use of AR technology is retail websites that allow a shopper to "try on" different pieces of clothing,[6] or "decorate" their room with furniture before buying.[7] Augmented reality is also used to allow field technicians or factory workers to overlay digital images showing how a piece of equipment should look, or instructions for how to repair a part, onto their current physical setting, either through a special screen or smart glasses.[8] The "metaverse" is a more recent development that comprises a networked set of computer-generated spaces, in which users can interact with both digital representations of systems and with each other, typically via an avatar.

Until recently, participating in the metaverse in a meaningful way typically required using a special headset and handheld controllers. However, as some companies push to bring the metaverse to fruition, many firms acknowledge the impracticality of asking people to purchase and use a headset, especially as part of their workday.

According to Leslie Shannon, a trend-scouting executive at telecommunications firm Nokia, and the author of a 2023 book on the metaverse, this has led work-related metaverse developers to shift away from spaces requiring headsets. Developers now favor spaces that people can access on any personal computer.[9] While not as rich or immersive as their headset-based counterparts, these spaces make the metaverse more appealing and accessible spaces for getting work done.[10]

One way to think about immersive technologies focuses on the high amount of sensory information they provide to the user (particularly in the case of virtual reality with headsets). But another definition of immersive technology focuses on the *results* of this heightened sensory experience, often described as a feeling of virtual "presence." Presence is a sense of immersion and realism that we get when physically in a location; virtual presence gives us a somewhat similar feeling, making us feel like we are actually somewhere else.[11]

It is this sense of presence that makes immersive technologies potentially exciting for remote work. Immersion and presence can help companies develop what employees and employers want, quality work without a sense of alienation—by allowing people to experience the casual interactions of real work, observe the body language of colleagues, and even do the physical tasks that now require a physical presence for many jobs—all from any location in the world.

According to Shannon, a remote worker can use a metaverse-based office application to experience presence in a virtual office as well as social presence at a level not usually possible through text or video-based communication. Workers, represented by avatars, can enter virtual offices, which can look identical to their physical offices. After employees enter the virtual space, they can seek each other out, or even encounter each other serendipitously, and engage in spontaneous interactions like those that people might find in a physical office. Because of the avatar-based virtual presence, these interactions theoretically can occur more organically than planned interactions via traditional remote work technologies.[12]

Technology consulting firm Accenture rolled out a global corporate metaverse for its employees in 2021, called The Nth Floor. The metaverse contains a virtual office called "One Accenture Park," which the company uses for onboarding new employees, training, and other virtual events. The space also includes replicas of several real-world Accenture offices where remote employees can meet up virtually and collaborate.[13] US firm Virbela has been providing metaverse workspaces to companies since before the pandemic[14] Similarly, South Korean technology firm Zigbang developed a metaverse called Soma that includes multiple offices and meeting spaces and can be used by companies or groups of workers for virtual interactions.[15] As both headset technology and internet bandwidth improve, it is likely that virtual office settings—now a novelty—will become a more common part of remote work.

Advances in remote manufacturing also mean that immersive technology may make many more types of jobs, including manufacturing, remote. Some tasks that workers historically performed in person on the shop floor can now be done remotely because of augmented or virtual reality, often with the aid of a digital twin on the manufacturing line.

Global firms, such as Unilever, have been working to develop remote manufacturing for years to centralize production line management and fine-tune supply chains.[16] However, the pandemic hastened further investment in remote technologies so that plants could work with fewer people on-site.

How do machine learning and artificial intelligence support remote and virtual work?

Many of the latest technological advances are the product of machine learning (the use of algorithms to teach computers to recognize patterns in data), and other artificial intelligence (AI) tools, which can (at least partly) simulate human intelligence to complete tasks. People can use these technologies to improve the remote and virtual work experience.

One of the most compelling examples of this trend is the use of AI to provide real-time administrative assistance and analytics in virtual meetings.[17] For example, one startup firm, Headroom, has a product that uses voice and facial recognition to transcribe video meetings and provide basic analytics on the participation levels of each member and the overall energy of the group, all in real-time, as the meeting goes on.[18] Some firms, such as Sembly, go deeper into documentation and use AI to generate a meeting summary after it has ended. The Sembly AI program also distributes and integrates meeting documentation into a firm's workflow. Other firms, such as Riff Analytics, focus more on conversation, using AI to generate an intensive analysis of team member participation and overall team dynamics. If used appropriately, these types of analytics can help teams improve their productivity and use time more efficiently.

What makes someone a digital nomad and is this a sustainable lifestyle?

The term "digital nomad" refers to someone who travels while working remotely. Digital nomadism is basically an extreme version of work from anywhere; not only can these workers move far away from their company location, they can also continue to travel between different locations while they work the same job.

The number of digital nomads is unknown, but in the United States alone it is likely in the millions.[19] The category comprises a wide range of workers in different situations, including both independent contractors (such as freelancers and independent consultants) and traditional company employees. Digital nomads may travel for part or all of a given year. They may also settle in another location for some time. While their travels often take them across country borders, some digital nomads travel within the same country.[20]

Despite their self-identified status as nomads, such people also seek social connections and have formed longstanding communities in far-flung places like Bali and parts of Thailand.[21] In response to this trend toward community-building, some companies and local governments have built communal residence and workspace centers targeting digital nomads in locations ranging from Medellín to London.[22] But even when a digital nomad remains in one place for an extended time, they still earn their income from another location, and they are not full participants in the local economy.

Digital nomads can be a boon to the economy of the place where they live because their income originates elsewhere (and they do not take jobs from local residents) but they spend money locally. Recognizing this, some countries offer special visas structured to attract digital nomads for periods typically ranging from six months up to as much as two years. While this practice is not new, it increased dramatically during the COVID-19 pandemic. Nearly fifty countries now offer some sort of digital nomad visa.[23]

Digital nomad life may sound appealing, but it also brings significant challenges. Accounts of current and former digital nomads describe a life full of travel, adventure, and new experiences, combined with bouts of loneliness, logistical snafus (particularly challenges with internet access), safety concerns, and financial pressures.[24]

While "digital nomad families"—digital nomads who bring home-schooled children along with them—may be more common post-pandemic, the evidence as to their real numbers is unclear. The effect of such a lifestyle on children is also uncertain. While many workers do enjoy great lifestyle benefits from the freedom to do their jobs remotely while traveling wherever they prefer, child-development experts caution that the lack of routine and regular connections with people outside the family over a longer period of time can be harmful to children.[25] As older children become more independent and have opportunities to join extracurricular activities, play sports, and make friends, the upside of the nomadic lifestyle may not offset the cost of losing out on a more traditional childhood. There are a few accounts of digital nomad parents traveling with teens who finish high school online, but these are rare compared to stories of digital nomad parents with small children.[26]

Do some remote employees work more than one job at the same time?

One of the more curious developments of an increase in remote work is that employers occasionally find out their workers are doing another, ostensibly full-time, job simultaneously. Most companies can't monitor the time remote employees spend actually working on particular tasks during the day so some workers can just take meetings and do tasks for another company while still collecting a salary from the first. While the exact numbers are difficult to estimate, the pandemic appears to have added to the number of people doing two full-time remote jobs at the same time, in a practice called "overemployment."

While it is conceivable that a remote employee could meet expectations at more than one employer, and thus they could hold down more than one job at the same time without problems, the level of apparent deception this requires, not to mention the apparent preoccupation of the employee with another position, is troublesome. A *Wall Street Journal* article describes one overemployed tech worker who "spends his days switching off among three laptops—work, personal, other work—keeping the one for his new job synced up to a desktop monitor and his other work computer open beside it . . . when [he] gets called on simultaneously in both meetings—it happens— he drops one call, answers the other's query and then pops back onto the 'dropped' call. Sorry, he had a network issue. What was the question again?"[27]

Working two full-time jobs is technically legal in most situations. The ethics of doing this, however, are shaky at best. Some employment contracts specify the employer's expectation that the employee will not take a second job.[28] Employees doing multiple remote jobs risk being fired by one or both employers, especially if the jobs pay annual salaries rather than hourly wages or if they are trying to fit more than one job into a normal forty-hour workweek. The fact that most employees engaged in such arrangements end up hiding one employer from the other, and often lie about their use of time during work hours, further underscores the problematic ethics and risks of firing.[29]

But there's been a more significant—and less controversial—second job development in recent years. Americans created record numbers of new businesses during the pandemic. There were five million new company applications in 2022, up 44 percent over 2019.[30] Some investors and experts who work with startups say that this increase appears to be driven partly by increased startup businesses run by people with full-time jobs.[31] They attribute this trend to the rise of remote work, which has given people more time (by eliminating commutes) and flexibility to pursue side businesses while still working for an employer.

While there is likely some overlap between these "side startup" remote workers and the truly overemployed, in general, these businesses appear to impinge much less on the worker's primary job, in part because they are often related to a hobby or other passion of the founder. For example, online marketplace Etsy reported a 28 percent year-over-year increase in the number of registered sellers in 2021, and a 109 percent increase over the period from 2019 to 2021; however, sellers realized average annual gross sales of only $2,302 in 2021.[32] These statistics represent a wave of new businesses that might supplement income for some, and eventually become a sole occupation for a few, but that largely represent fulfillment of a side passion, rather than true overemployment.

Can we expect companies to go all-remote, with no offices at all?

After governments began easing pandemic lockdowns, many companies announced that they were becoming permanently remote, allowing remote work for most or all employees indefinitely. But this is different from all-remote, in which the company has no office space at all.

Even before the pandemic, there have been intriguing examples of organizations that run entirely virtually, with no physical offices. Unsurprisingly, most all-remote companies are either technology or services firms in which the main types of work lend themselves well to a remote setting.[33]

The most visible of these is GitLab, a software-development platform provider that has been all-remote since its founding in 2011. As of early 2023, GitLab had more than two thousand employees in sixty-five countries. And no company offices. GitLab has long touted its all-remote approach as a critical piece of its operating model, and it has a full-time "Head of Remote" position in its executive ranks. The firm makes publicly available a "Guide to All-Remote," in which it outlines its philosophy of all-remote working and describes operating procedures that can help other companies put this approach into practice. GitLab also makes public its own company handbook, which lists all its company policies and processes in great detail, including a substantial section on remote work.[34]

GitLab is not the only all-remote company—others include Zapier, Automattic, and Quora—but it claims (and appears) to be the largest firm to use this model. There is no systematic tracking of all-remote companies, but all evidence suggests that most all-remote firms are small, with fewer than one hundred employees. While many companies have reduced their office space,[35] most of them still maintain physical offices. Even those organizations that have gone fully remote still generally retain at least a physical corporate headquarters.

While theoretically larger all-remote companies should be feasible, current behavior suggests that this format is unlikely to extend beyond small to mid-size companies in the foreseeable future.

Any final thoughts on the future of remote work?

In 1979, "founder of telecommuting" Jack Nilles had only been writing about remote work for a few years, and IBM had just begun its experiment sending work terminals to the homes of five employees. Someone looking several decades into the future at that time would likely have predicted that remote work could conceivably expand, if there were technology developed that enabled it. A world in which nearly half of the population spent at least some time working from home might have seemed theoretically possible, but practically speaking, unlikely. And yet, futuristic thinkers such as Nilles envisioned an environmentally sustainable utopia of remote work, which has proven to be elusive. As we look ahead to the next forty or fifty years, it is wise to keep that 1979 perspective in mind. Whatever the future holds for the workplace, it is likely that we will see some changes emerge that had previously appeared speculative at best, while other forecasted trends will fail to materialize.

The safest prediction of the future of remote work is that it will be driven by the needs of both employers and employees, rather than evolving in a technological or policy bubble. New technologies, such as the metaverse, will only be adopted at scale if they meaningfully improve the experience and the results of work. Remote work policies and practices will only survive if they support recruitment and retention of key talent.

During the pandemic years of 2020 to 2022, we saw an intensive period of experimentation with different practices and technologies. I expect that this experimentation will continue, but at a slower pace in the coming decades (barring another disruptive event such as the pandemic). Despite the remonstrations of some senior executives and other skeptics today, I also expect that remote work will be an ongoing feature of our workplace well into the future. I hope that after reading this book, you are looking forward to this future as much as I am.

NOTES

Chapter 1

1. Jack Nilles, "Telecommunications and Organizational Decentralization," *IEEE Transactions on Communications* 23, no. 10 (1975): 1142–1147, https://doi.org/10.1109/TCOM.1975.1092687.

2. Ed Berthiaume, "Jack Nilles Tried to Ignite a Work-from-Home Trend 48 Years Ago. It's Finally Here," Lawrence University, August 17, 2020, https://www.lawrence.edu/articles/lu-alum-jack-nilles-father-telecommuting.

3. Jack Nilles, *The Telecommunications–Transportation Tradeoff: Options for Tomorrow* (Charleston, SC: BookSurge Publishing, 2007).

4. Nilles, "Telecommunications and Organizational Decentralization."

5. Janet Caldow, "Working Outside the Box: A Study of the Growing Momentum in Telework," white paper, IBM Institute for Electronic Government, 2009.

6. Caldow, "Working Outside the Box."

7. Kerry Elizabeth Knobelsdorff, "Telecommuting: Reality Sets In," *Christian Science Monitor*, June 8, 1987, https://www.csmonitor.com/1987/0608/ftelly.html.

8. Unless otherwise cited, statistics in this chapter for the prevalence of remote and hybrid work in the United States come from WFH Research and are attributed to Jose Maria

Barrero, Nicholas Bloom, and Steven J. Davis, "Why Working from Home Will Stick," National Bureau of Economic Research Working Paper 28731 (2021), https://doi.org/10.3386/w28731.

9. "Intranets.com Sold to WebEx for $45M," *Boston Business Journal*, August 1, 2005, https://www.bizjournals.com/boston/stories/2005/08/01/daily14.html.

10. John Stein Monroe, "4 Reasons Why Managers Resist Telework and Why They Might Be Wrong," *Federal Computer Week*, September 4, 2010, https://fcw.com/workforce/2010/09/4-reasons-why-managers-resist-telework-and-why-they-might-be-wrong/223349/.

11. These concerns, among others, will be addressed in more detail in Chapter 4.

12. Kara Swisher, "Yahoo CEO Mayer Now Requiring Remote Employees to Not Be (Remote)," *All Things D*, February 22, 2013, https://allthingsd.com/20130222/yahoo-ceo-mayer-now-requiring-all-remote-employees-to-not-be-remote/index.html.

13. Kara Swisher, "'Physically Together': Here's the Internal Yahoo No-Work-From-Home Memo for Remote Workers and Maybe More," *All Things D*, February 22, 2013, https://allthingsd.com/20130222/physically-together-heres-the-internal-yahoo-no-work-from-home-memo-which-extends-beyond-remote-workers.

14. Jenna Goudreau, "Back to the Stone Age? New Yahoo CEO Marissa Mayer Bans Working from Home," *Forbes*, February 25, 2013, https://www.forbes.com/sites/jennagoudreau/2013/02/25/back-to-the-stone-age-new-yahoo-ceo-marissa-mayer-bans-working-from-home/?sh=2024793e1667; Emma G. Keller, "Yahoo CEO Marissa Mayer's Work-from-Home Memo Is from Bygone Era," *The Guardian*, February 26, 2013, https://www.theguardian.com/commentisfree/2013/feb/26/yahoo-ceo-marissa-mayer-memo-telecomute.

15. Julianne Pepitone, "Best Buy Ends Work-from-Home Program," *CNN Business*, March 5, 2013, https://money.cnn.

com/2013/03/05/technology/best-buy-work-from-home/;
Alice Truong, "Reddit Gives Remote Employees until End
of Year to Relocate to San Francisco," *Fast Company*, October
3, 2014, https://www.fastcompany.com/3036660/reddit-
gives-remote-employees-until-end-of-year-to-relocate-to-san-
francisco.

16. Caroline Humer, "In Telecommuting Debate, Aetna Sticks
by Big At-Home Workforce," *Reuters*, March 1, 2013,
https://www.reuters.com/article/us-yahoo-telecommut
ing-aetna/in-telecommuting-debate-aetna-sticks-by-big-at-
home-workforce-idUSBRE92006820130301; "Aetna to Cut
Workforce, Reduce Work-at-Home Policy," *Hartford Courant*,
October 12, 2016, https://www.courant.com/business/hc-
aetna-work-at-home-20161010-story.html.

17. Chris Isidore, "IBM Tells Employees Working at Home to
Get Back to the Office," *CNN Business*, May 19, 2017, https://
money.cnn.com/2017/05/19/technology/ibm-work-at-
home/index.html.

18. Dana Wilkie, "When Remote Work 'Works' for Employees,
but Not the C-Suite," *SHRM*, April 10, 2017, https://www.
shrm.org/resourcesandtools/hr-topics/employee-relations/
pages/remote-work-.aspx.

19. Barrero, Bloom, and Davis, "Why Working from Home Will
Stick."

20. Barrero, Bloom, and Davis, "Why Working from Home Will
Stick."

21. Cevat Giray Aksoy et al., "Working from Home around the
World," Brookings Papers on Economic Activity, September
7, 2022, https://www.brookings.edu/bpea-articles/working-
from-home-around-the-world/.

22. Clive Thompson, "What If Working from Home Goes
On . . . Forever?" *New York Times*, June 9, 2020, https://www.
nytimes.com/interactive/2020/06/09/magazine/remote-
work-covid.html.

23. Francis Agustin, "Salesforce's Marc Benioff Says In-Person
Office Attendance Is Low because Employees Are 'So

Productive at Home,'" *Business Insider*, August 26, 2021, https://www.businessinsider.com/salesforce-ceo-says-work ers-are-just-as-productive-at-home-2021-8.

24. Sridhar Natarajan and Shahien Nasiripour, "Goldman CEO's Year of Empty Offices, Island Getaways and Strife," *Bloomberg*, March 14, 2021, https://www.bloomberg.com/ news/articles/2021-03-14/goldman-ceo-s-year-of-empty-offi ces-island-getaways-and-strife?sref=1kJVNqnU&leadSource= uverify%20wall#xj4y7vzkg.

25. Joshua Franklin, "The Reinvention of Goldman Sachs: What Has David Solomon Achieved?" *Financial Times*, August 17, 2022, https://www.ft.com/content/30c61d67-8af9-474e-872a-b0c75258a781.

26. David Miller and Haley Yamada, "The Great Resignation: Its Origins and What It Means for Future Business," *ABC News*, May 3, 2022, https://abcnews.go.com/US/great-resignation-origins-means-future-business/story?id=84222583.

27. The Conference Board, "Is the Office Dying? Of Those Who Quit during the Pandemic, One in Four Did So for the Flexibility to Work from Anywhere," press release, December 2, 2021, https://www.conference-board.org/press/Rapid-respose-Dec-21.

28. Bureau of Labor Statistics, "Job Flexibilities and Work Schedules Summary," Economic News Release, September 24, 2019, https://www.bls.gov/news.release/flex2.nr0.htm; *Telecommuting Trend Data* (Carlsbad, CA: Global Workplace Analytics, 2021), https://globalworkplaceanalytics.com/ telecommuting-statistics.

29. Barrero, Bloom, and Davis, "Why Working from Home Will Stick."

30. "WeWork Expects 2022 Revenue to Jump at Least 30% on Office Space Demand," *Reuters*, March 11, 2022, https:// www.reuters.com/business/wework-reports-smaller-fourth-quarter-loss-cost-cuts-office-space-demand-2022-03-11/.

31. For example, Bureau of Labor Statistics, "American Times Use Survey—2018 Results," News Release, June 19, 2019,

Table 6, https://www.bls.gov/news.release/archives/atus_0
6192019.pdf.

32. Barrero, Bloom, and Davis, "Why Working from Home Will
    Stick."

33. Emily Courtney, "Why Do Some Remote Jobs Require a
    Location?" *Flexjobs*, https://www.flexjobs.com/blog/post/
    why-do-some-remote-jobs-require-a-location/. Flexjobs
    indicates that 95 percent of remote job postings have some
    geographic requirements, whether a specific metro area or a
    specific country.

34. Jessica Howington, "Top 30 Companies That Hire for Work-
    from-Anywhere Jobs," *Flexjobs*, https://www.flexjobs.com/
    blog/post/top-companies-work-from-anywhere-remote-
    jobs/.

35. One example of this discussion is found in Klas Rönnbäck,
    "Transaction Costs of Early Modern Multinational
    Enterprise: Measuring the Transatlantic Information Lag of
    the British Royal African Company and its Successor, 1680–
    1818," *Business History* 58, no. 8 (2016): 1147–1163, https://
    doi.org/10.1080/00076791.2016.1156087.

Chapter 2

1. Lee Sproull and Sara Kiesler, "Reducing Social Context
   Cues: Electronic Mail in Organizational Communication,"
   Management Science 32, no. 11 (1986): 1492–1512, https://
   doi.org/10.1287/mnsc.32.11.1492; Jane Siegel et al., "Group
   Processes in Computer-Mediated Communication,"
   Organizational Behavior and Human Decision Processes
   37, no. 2 (1986): 157–187, https://doi.org/10.1016/
   0749-5978(86)90050-6.

2. Daantje Derks, Agneta H. Fischer, and Arjan E. R. Bos, "The
   Role of Emotion in Computer-mediated Communication: A
   Review," *Computers in Human Behavior* 24, no. 3 (2008): 766–
   785, https://doi.org/10.1016/j.chb.2007.04.004.

3. "Communication and Conflict in a Virtual World," August 13,
   2020, National Institutes of Health, Office of the Ombudsman,

https://ombudsman.nih.gov/content/communication-and-conflict-virtual-world.

4. Aaron McDade, "Applebee's Franchise Executive Fired after Email Justifying Lower Pay," *Newsweek*, March 29, 2022, https://www.newsweek.com/applebees-executive-fired-after-suggesting-inflation-justifies-lower-pay-1693125.

5. Matthew Green, "No Comment! Why More News Sites Are Dumping Their Comment Sections," *KQED*, January 24, 2018, https://www.kqed.org/lowdown/29720/no-comment-why-a-growing-number-of-news-sites-are-dumping-their-comment-sections; Jeffrey Goldberg, "We Want to Hear from You," *The Atlantic*, February 2, 2018, https://www.theatlantic.com/letters/archive/2018/02/we-want-to-hear-from-you/552170/.

6. Laura Hazard Owen, "With Corgis, Chickens, and Kitchen Reveals, the NYT Cooking Community Facebook Group Is a 'Happy Corner of the Internet,'" *Neiman Lab*, April 17, 2019, https://www.niemanlab.org/2019/04/with-corgis-chickens-and-kitchen-reveals-the-nyt-cooking-community-facebook-group-is-a-happy-corner-of-the-internet/; Lauren Strapagiel, "The *New York Times* Is Giving Up Its Cooking Community Facebook Group with over 77,000 Members," *BuzzFeed News*, March 18, 2021, https://www.buzzfeednews.com/article/laurenstrapagiel/the-new-york-times-is-abandoning-its-cooking-facebook-group.

7. Lindy West, "What Happened When I Confronted My Cruellest Troll," *The Guardian*, February 2, 2015, https://www.theguardian.com/society/2015/feb/02/what-happened-confronted-cruellest-troll-lindy-west.

8. Arlin Cuncic, "The Psychology of Cyberbullying," *Verywell Mind*, February 19, 2022, https://www.verywellmind.com/the-psychology-of-cyberbullying-5086615.

9. Gabrielle Bienasz, "Shopify Reportedly Appoints 'Channel Champions' and Shuts Down Slack Channels When Conversations Get Heated," *Entrepreneur*, August 31, 2022, https://www.entrepreneur.com/business-news/

this-is-how-shopify-is-reportedly-monitoring-slack-chann els/434484; Jennings Brown, "Harassment, Transphobia, and Racism: A Look Inside Blind's Anonymous Chatting Forum for Google Employees," *Gizmodo*, January 31, 2019, https://gizmodo.com/harassment-transphobia-and-racism-a-look-inside-blin-1831999239.

10. Shane Snow, "Anonymity: The Secret Killer of Company Culture," *Ladders News*, May 27, 2019, https://www.the ladders.com/career-advice/anonymity-the-secret-killer-of-company-culture; Jodi Kantor and David Streitfeld, "Inside Amazon: Wrestling Big Ideas in a Bruising Workplace," *New York Times*, August 15, 2015, https://www.nytimes.com/2015/08/16/technology/inside-amazon-wrestling-big-ideas-in-a-bruising-workplace.html.

11. Yaacov Trope and Nira Liberman, "Construal-Level Theory of Psychological Distance," *Psychological Review* 117, no. 2 (2010): 440, https://doi.org/10.1037/a0018963.

12. Jeanne M. Wilson et al., "Perceived Proximity in Virtual Work: Explaining the Paradox of Far-But-Close," *Organization Studies* 29, no. 7 (2008): 979–1002, https://doi.org/10.1177/0170840607083105; Jeanne Wilson, C. Brad Crisp, and Mark Mortensen, "Extending Construal-Level Theory to Distributed Groups: Understanding the Effects of Virtuality," *Organization Science* 24, no. 2 (2012): 629–644, https://doi.org/10.1287/orsc.1120.0750.

13. Catherine Durnell Cramton, "The Mutual Knowledge Problem and Its Consequences for Dispersed Collaboration," *Organization Science* 12, no. 3 (2001): 346–371, https://doi.org/10.1287/orsc.12.3.346.10098.

14. Catherine Durnell Cramton, Kara L. Orvis, and Jeanne M. Wilson, "Situation Invisibility and Attribution in Distributed Collaborations, *Journal of Management* 33, no. 4 (2007): 525–546, https://doi.org/10.1177/0149206307302549.

15. Cecily D. Cooper and Nancy B. Kurland, "Telecommuting, Professional Isolation, and Employee Development in Public and Private Organizations," *Journal of Organizational Behavior*

23, no. 4 (2002): 511–532, https://doi.org/10.1002/job.145; Timothy D. Golden and Sumita Raghuram, "Teleworker Knowledge Sharing and the Role of Altered Relational and Technological Interactions," *Journal of Organizational Behavior* 31, no. 8 (2010): 1061–1085, https://doi.org/10.1002/job.652.

16. Siegel et al., "Group Processes."
17. Sara Kiesler, Jane Siegel, and Timothy McGuire, "Social Psychological Aspects of Computer-Mediated Communication," *American Psychologist* 39, no. 10 (1984): 1123–1134, https://doi.org/10.1037/0003-066X.39.10.1123.
18. Susan G. Straus, "Getting a Clue: The Effects of Communication Media and Information Distribution on Participation and Performance in Computer-Mediated and Face-to-Face Groups," *Small Group Research* 27, no. 1 (1986): 115–142, https://doi.org/10.1177/1046496496271006.
19. Radostina Purvanova et al., "Who Emerges into Virtual Team Leadership Roles? The Role of Achievement and Ascription Antecedents for Leadership Emergence across the Virtuality Spectrum," *Journal of Business and Psychology* 36, no. 4 (2021): 713–733, https//doi.org/10.1007/s10869-020-09698-0.
20. Dale L. Goodhue, "Understanding User Evaluations of Information Systems," *Management Science* 41, no. 12 (1995): 1827–1844, https://doi.org/10.1287/mnsc.41.12.1827; Dale L. Goodhue and Ronald L. Thompson, "Task-Technology Fit and Individual Performance," *MIS Quarterly* 19, no. 2 (1995): 213–236, https://doi.org/10.2307/249689.
21. Jane Their, "'Weak, Pathetic, and Cruel': HR Managers Weigh In on Elon Musk's Twitter Mass Layoffs," *Fortune*, November 8, 2022, https://fortune.com/2022/11/08/elon-musk-twitter-mass-layoff-cruel-human-resources-managers/.
22. Kurt Wagner and Edward Ludlow, "Twitter Now Asks Some Fired Workers to Please Come Back," *Bloomberg News*, November 6, 2022, https://www.bloomberg.com/news/articles/2022-11-06/twitter-now-asks-some-fired-workers-to-please-come-back.

23. Shira Li Bartov, "Restaurant Worker Fired via email from 'Coward' Boss 20 Minutes after Shift," *Newsweek*, July 18, 2022, https://www.newsweek.com/restaurant-worker-fired-via-email-coward-boss-20-minutes-after-shift-1725583.

24. Jill Purdy, Pete Nye, and P. V. Balakrishnan, "The Impact of Communication Media on Negotiation Outcomes," *International Journal of Conflict Management* 1, no. 2 (2000): 162–187, https://doi.org/10.1108/eb022839.

Chapter 3

1. Nicholas Bloom et al., "Does Working from Home Work? Evidence from a Chinese Experiment," *Quarterly Journal of Economics* 130, no. 1 (2015): 165–218, https://doi.org/10.3386/w18871.

2. Prithwiraj (Raj) Choudhury, Cirrus Foroughi, and Barbara Larson, "Work-from-Anywhere: The Productivity Effects of Geographic Flexibility," *Strategic Management Journal* 42, no. 4 (2021): 655–683, https://doi.org/10.1002/smj.3251.

3. Patent examiners are professionals who determine whether an invention is sufficiently original to warrant a patent. They are typically college-educated, often with degrees in relevant subjects, such as engineering or the sciences.

4. Kate Conger, "Facebook Starts Planning for Permanent Remote Workers," *New York Times*, May 21, 2020, https://www.nytimes.com/2020/05/21/technology/facebook-remote-work-coronavirus.html.

5. Guido Hertel, Susanne Geister, and Udo Konradt, "Managing Virtual Teams: A Review of Current Empirical Research," *Human Resource Management Review* 15, no. 1 (2005): 69–95, https://doi.org/10.1016/j.hrmr.2005.01.002.

6. Thomas A. O'Neill, Laura A. Hambley, and Gina S. Chatellier, "Cyberslacking, Engagement, and Personality in Distributed Work Environments," *Computers in Human Behavior* 40 (2014): 152–160, https://doi.org/10.1016/j.chb.2014.08.005.

7. Alexander S. Dennis, Jordan B. Barlow, and Alan R. Dennis, "The Power of Introverts: Personality and Intelligence in

Virtual Teams," *Journal of Management Information Systems* 39, no. 1 (2022): 102–129, https://doi.org/10.1080/07421 222.2021.2023408; Maria Charalampous et al., "Systematically Reviewing Remote e-Workers' Well-Being at Work: A Multidimensional Approach," *European Journal of Work and Organisational Psychology* 28, no. 1 (2019): 51–73, https://doi.org/10.1080/1359432X.2018.1541886.

8. Leigh Anne Clark, Steven J. Karau, and Michael D. Michalisin, "Telecommuting Attitudes and the 'Big Five' Personality Dimensions," *Journal of Management Policy and Practice* 13 (2012): 31–46.

9. Pascale Peters, Kea G. Tijdens, and Cécile Wetzels, "Employees' Opportunities, Preferences, and Practices in Telecommuting Adoption," *Information & Management* 41, no. 4 (2004): 469–482, https://doi.org/10.1016/S0378-7206(03)00085-5. Some surveys conducted during the height of pandemic restrictions found that women reported a lower preference for remote work than men, but this appears to be due more to impingement from family on work time in the lockdown setting and is likely not representative of pre- and post-pandemic preferences.

10. Timothy D. Golden, John F. Veiga, and Zeki Simsek, "Telecommuting's Differential Impact on Work-Family Conflict: Is There No Place Like Home?" *Journal of Applied Psychology* 91, no. 6 (2006): 1340–1350. https://doi.org/10.1037/0021-9010.91.6.1340; Peters, Tijdens, and Wetzels, "Employees' Opportunities, Preferences, and Practices."

11. Hani Hahmassani et al., "Employee Attitudes and Stated Preferences Toward Telecommuting: An Exploratory Analysis," *Transportation Research Record* 1413 (1993): 31.

12. "HBS Online Survey Shows Most Professionals Have Excelled While Working from Home," *HBS Online*, March 25, 2022, https://online.hbs.edu/blog/post/fut ure-of-work-from-home.

13. Kristen M. Shockley and Tammy D. Allen, "Motives for Flexible Work Arrangement Use," *Community, Work & Family*

15, no. 2 (2012): 217–231, https://doi.org/10.1080/13668
803.2011.609661.

14. Bureau of Labor Statistics, *American Time Use Survey News Release*, press release, July 22, 2021, https://www.bls.
gov/news.release/archives/atus_07222021.htm; Jaclyn S.
Wong and Andrew M. Penner, "Gender and the Returns
to Attractiveness," *Research in Social Stratification and Mobility* 44 (2016): 113–123, https://doi.org/10.1016/
j.rssm.2016.04.002.

15. *Gender Bias in Workplace Culture Curbs Careers*, Murray
Edwards College, https://www.murrayedwards.cam.
ac.uk/about/womens-voices-womens-future/collaborat
ing-with-men.

16. Ruchika Tulshyan, "Return to Office? Some Women of Color
Aren't Ready," *New York Times*, June 23, 2021, https://www.
nytimes.com/2021/06/23/us/return-to-office-anxiety.html.

17. Eugene Robinson, "Of Course Many People of Color Prefer
Remote Work. It Helps Dodge Office Weirdness," *Los Angeles Times*, April 3, 2022, https://www.latimes.com/opinion/
story/2022-04-03/work-from-home-race-office.

18. Erica Pandey, "Women, People of Color Happier Working
from Home," *Axios*, February 22, 2022, https://www.axios.
com/2022/02/22/unequal-return-office-hybrid-women-peo
ple-of-color.

19. Patricia Mokhtarian and Ilan Salomon, "Modeling the Desire
to Telecommute: The Importance of Attitudinal Factors in
Behavioral Models," *Transportation Research Part A: Policy and Practice* 31, no. 1 (1997): 35–50, https://doi.org/10.1016/
S0965-8564(96)00010-9.

20. France Bélanger, "Workers' Propensity to
Telecommute: An Empirical Study," *Information & Management* 35, no. 3 (1999): 139–153, https://doi.or/
10.1016/S0378-7206(98)00091-3.

21. "Americans Are Embracing Flexible Work—And
They Want More of It," McKinsey & Company, June
23, 2022, https://www.mckinsey.com/industries/

real-estate/our-insights/americans-are-embracing-flexi
ble-work-and-they-want-more-of-it.

22. Sara Fischer and Jennifer A. Kingson, "Millennials Drive Remote Work Push," *Axios*, May 24, 2022, https://www.axios.com/2022/05/24/millennials-drive-remote-work-push.

23. Fischer and Kingson, "Millennials Drive Remote Work."

24. United States Census Bureau, *Census Bureau Estimates Show Average One-Way Travel Time to Work Rises to All-Time High*, press release number CB21-TPS.29, March 18, 2021, https://www.census.gov/newsroom/press-releases/2021/one-way-travel-time-to-work-rises.html.

25. Paula Caligiuri and Helen De Cieri, "Predictors of Employees' Preference for Working from Home Post-pandemic," *Business and Economic Research* 11, no. 2 (2021): 1–19, https://doi.org/10.5296/ber.v11i2.18411.

26. Peters, Tijdens, and Wetzels, "Employees' Opportunities, Preferences, and Practices."

27. American Psychiatric Association, "As Americans Begin to Return to the Office, Views on Workplace Mental Health Are Mixed," press release, May 20, 2021, https://www.psychiatry.org/newsroom/news-releases/as-americans-begin-to-return-to-the-office-views-on-workplace-mental-health-are-mixed.

28. Bloom et al., "Does Working from Home Work?"

29. Larson, Makarius, and Wilk, Research in progress.

30. Timothy D. Golden, John F. Veiga, and Richard N. Dino, "The Impact of Professional Isolation on Teleworker Job Performance and Turnover Intentions: Does Time Spent Teleworking, Interacting Face-to-Face, or Having Access to Communication-enhancing Technology Matter?" *Journal of Applied Psychology* 93, no. 6 (2008): 1412–1421, https://doi.org/10.1037/a0012722.

31. Blythe Renay, Message in the discussion "Why Do People Work 'Remotely' From Coffee Shops?" *Quora*, January 27, 2021, https://www.quora.com/Why-do-people-work-remotely-from-coffee-shops.

32. Vivek Nair, Message in the discussion "Why Do People Work 'Remotely' From Coffee Shops?" *Quora*, January 10, 2020, https://www.quora.com/Why-do-people-work-remotely-from-coffee-shops.

33. Ravi S. Gajendran and David A. Harrison, "The Good, the Bad, and the Unknown about Telecommuting: Meta-Analysis of Psychological Mediators and Individual Consequences," *Journal of Applied Psychology* 92, no. 6 (2007): 1524–1541, https://doi.org/10.1037/0021-9010.92.6.1524; Golden, Veiga, and Simsek, "Telecommuting's Differential Impact."

34. Timothy D. Golden and John F. Veiga, "The Impact of Extent of Telecommuting on Job Satisfaction: Resolving Inconsistent Findings," *Journal of Management* 31, no. 2 (2005): 301–318, https://doi.org/10.1177/0149206304271768; Golden, Veiga, and Simsek, "Telecommuting's Differential Impact."

35. Tammy D. Allen, Timothy D. Golden, and Kristen M. Shockley, "How Effective Is Telecommuting? Assessing the Status of Our Scientific Findings," *Psychological Science in the Public Interest* 16, no. 2 (2015): 40–68, https://doi.org/10.1177/1529100615593273.

36 Mary C. Noonan and Jennifer L. Glass, "The Hard Truth about Telecommuting," *Monthly Labor Review* 135 (2012): 38–45.

37. Cali Morrison, "How to Work Remotely When Your Office Closes for Coronavirus—Or Any Time," *EdSurge*, March 10, 2020, https://www.edsurge.com/news/2020-03-10-how-to-work-remotely-when-your-office-closes-for-coronavirus-or-any-time.

38. Barrero, Bloom, and Davis, "Why Working from Home Will Stick."

39. Bloom et al., "Does Working from Home Work?"

40. Society for Human Resource Management (SHRM), *SHRM Research Reveals Negative Perceptions of Remote Work*, press release, July 26, 2021, https://www.shrm.org/about-shrm/press-room/press-releases/pages/-shrm-research-reveals-negative-perceptions-of-remote-work.aspx.

41. Scott E. Seibert, Michael J. Crant, and Maria L. Kraimer, "Proactive Personality and Career Success," *Journal of Applied Psychology* 84, no. 3 (1999): 416–427, doi:10.1037/0021-9010.84.3.416.

42. Duncan Wardle, "How to Network in the Age of Remote Work," *Harvard Business Review*, November 23, 2022, https://hbr.org/2022/11/how-to-network-in-the-age-of-remote-work.

43. Ray A. Smith, "Yes, You Can Find a Mentor While Working Remotely," *Wall Street Journal*, January 27, 2022, https://www.wsj.com/articles/new-school-way-to-find-mentor-when-doing-remote-work-11643290156.

Chapter 4

1. Bradford S. Bell and Steve W. J. Kozlowski, "A Typology of Virtual Teams: Implications for Effective Leadership," *Group & Organization Management* 27, no. 1 (2002): 14–49, https://doi.org/10.1177/1059601102027001003.

2. Sharon K. Parker, Caroline Knight, and Anita Keller, "Remote Managers Are Having Trust Issues," *Harvard Business Review*, July 30, 2020, https://hbr.org/2020/07/remote-managers-are-having-trust-issues.

3. Bradford S. Bell, Kristie L. McAlpine, and N. Sharon Hill, "Leading Virtually," *Annual Review of Organizational Psychology and Organizational Behavior* 10 (2023): 339–362, https://doi.org/10.1146/annurev-orgpsych-120920-050115.

4. Raghu Krishnamoorthy, "What Great Remote Managers Do Differently," *Harvard Business Review*, October 26, 2022, https://hbr.org/2022/10/what-great-remote-managers-do-differently.

5. Krishnamoorthy, "What Great Remote Managers Do Differently."

6. J. Richard Hackman and Greg R. Oldham, "Motivation through the Design of Work: Test of a Theory," *Organizational Behavior and Human Performance* 16, no. 2 (1976): 250–279, https://doi.org/10.1016/0030-5073(76)90016-7.

7. Timothy D. Golden and John F. Veiga, "The Impact of Superior–Subordinate Relationships on the Commitment, Job Satisfaction, and Performance of Virtual Workers," *The Leadership Quarterly* 19, no. 1 (2008): 77–88, https://doi.org/10.1016/j.leaqua.2007.12.009.

8. For example, Cecily D. Cooper and Nancy B. Kurland, "Telecommuting, Professional Isolation, and Employee Development in Public and Private Organizations," *Journal of Organizational Behavior* 23, no. 4 (2002): 511–532, https://doi.org/10.1002/job.145; Pamela J. Hinds and Catherine Durnell Cramton, "Situated Coworker Familiarity: How Site Visits Transform Relationships among Distributed Workers," *Organization Science* 25, no. 3 (2014): 794–814, https://doi.org/10.1287/orsc.2013.0869.

9. Timothy A. Judge, Ronald F. Piccolo, and Remus Ilies, "The Forgotten Ones? The Validity of Consideration and Initiating Structure in Leadership Research," *Journal of Applied Psychology* 89, no. 1 (2004): 36–51, https://doi.org/10.1037/0021-9010.89.1.36; Reinout E. de Vries, Angelique Bakker-Pieper, and Wyneke Oostenveld, "Leadership = Communication? The Relations of Leaders' Communication Styles with Leadership Styles, Knowledge Sharing and Leadership Outcomes," *Journal of Business and Psychology* 25, no. 3 (2010): 367–380, https://doi.org/10.1007/s10869-009-9140-2.

10. Batia M. Wiesenfeld, Sumita Raghuram, and Raghu Garud, "Organizational Identification among Virtual Workers: The Role of Need for Affiliation and Perceived Work-Based Social Support," *Journal of Management* 27, no. 2 (2001): 213–229, https://doi.org/10.1177/014920630102700205.

11. Thomas J. Peters and Robert H. Waterman, Jr., *In Search of Excellence: Lessons from America's Best-Run Companies* (New York: Harper & Row, 1982), 289.

12. This passage is not intended as a criticism of managing by wandering around as a supervisory strategy; when done correctly, it can be an important source of support and

motivation for employees in an office setting. It does not, however, translate to a remote work setting effectively.

13. Chak Fu Lam et al., "The Impact of Feedback Frequency on Learning and Task Performance: Challenging the 'More Is Better' Assumption," *Organizational Behavior and Human Decision Processes* 116, no. 2 (2011): 217–228, https://doi.org/10.1016/j.obhdp.2011.05.002.

14. Rani Molla, "You're Going Back to the Office. Your Boss Isn't," *Vox*, October 12, 2022, https://www.vox.com/recode/2022/10/12/23400496/remote-work-from-home-office-boss-manager-hypocrisy.

15. "Executives Feel the Strain of Leading in the "New Normal," October 2022, 12, https://futureforum.com/research/pulse-report-fall-2022-executives-feel-strain-leading-in-new-normal/).

16. Edward E. Lawler, "Equity Theory as a Predictor of Productivity and Work Quality," *Psychological Bulletin* 70, no. 6 (1968): 596, https://doi.org/10.1037/h0026848.

17. Barbara Z. Larson, "Give Your Remote Team Unstructured Time for Collaboration," *Harvard Business Review*, October 27, 2020, https://hbr.org/2020/10/give-your-remote-team-unstructured-time-for-collaboration.

18. A great example of this argument can be found in a 2022 *Fortune* article: Trey Williams, "Bosses Are Obsessed with Returning to the Office. Here's Why It's Already Out of Their Hands," *Fortune*, September 15, 2022, https://fortune.com/2022/09/15/why-are-bosses-obsessed-with-returning-to-the-office/.

Chapter 5

1. John E. Mathieu, Peter T. Gallagher, Monique A. Domingo, and Elizabeth A. Klock, "Embracing Complexity: Reviewing the Past Decade of Team Effectiveness Research," *Annual Review of Organizational Psychology and Organizational Behavior* 6 (2019): 17–46, https://doi.org/10.1146/annurev-orgpsych-012218-015106.

2. Erin E. Makarius and Barbara Z. Larson, "Changing the Perspective of Virtual Work: Building Virtual Intelligence at the Individual Level," *Academy of Management Perspectives* 31, no. 2 (2017): 159–178, https://doi.org/10.5465/amp.2014.0120.

3. Jennifer L. Gibbs, Anu Sivunen, and Maggie Boyraz, "Investigating the Impacts of Team Type and Design on Virtual Team Processes," *Human Resource Management Review* 27, no. 4 (2017): 590–603, https://doi.org/10.1016/j.hrmr.2016.12.006; Radostina K. Purvanova and Renata Kenda, "The Impact of Virtuality on Team Effectiveness in Organizational and Non-Organizational Teams: A Meta-Analysis," *Applied Psychology* 71, no. 3 (2022): 1082–1131, https://doi.org/10.1111/apps.12348.

4. Tsedal Neeley, "Global Teams That Work," *Harvard Business Review*, October 2015, https://hbr.org/2015/10/glo bal-teams-that-work.

5. Bradley L. Kirkman et al., "Five Challenges to Virtual Team Success: Lessons from Sabre, Inc." *Academy of Management Executive* 16, no. 3 (2002): 67–79, https://doi.org/10.5465/ame.2002.8540322.

6. Melanie S. Brucks and Jonathan Levav, "Virtual Communication Curbs Creative Idea Generation," *Nature* 605 (2022): 108–112, https://doi.org/10.1038/s41586-022-04643-y.

7. J. B. Walther, "Relational Aspects of Computer-Mediated Communication: Experimental Observations over Time," *Organization Science* 6, no. 2 (1995): 186–203, https://doi.org/10.1287/orsc.6.2.186; Sirkka L. Jarvenpaa, Kathleen Knoll, and Dorothy E. Leidner, "Is Anybody Out There? Antecedents of Trust in Global Virtual Teams," *Journal of Management Information Systems* 14, no. 4 (1998): 29–64, https://doi.org/10.1080/07421222.1998.11518185.

8. Catherine Durnell Cramton and Pamela J. Hinds, "An Embedded Model of Cultural Adaptation in Global Teams," *Organization Science* 25, no. 4 (2014): 1056–1081, https://doi.org/10.1287/orsc.2013.0885.

9. Jeffery A. LePine et al., "A Meta-Analysis of Teamwork Processes: Tests of a Multidimensional Model and Relationships with Team Effectiveness Criteria," *Personnel Psychology* 61, no. 2 (2008): 273–307, https://doi.org/10.1111/j.1744-6570.2008.00114.x.

10. Frank Siebdrat, Martin Hoegl, and Holger Ernst, "How to Manage Virtual Teams," *MIT Sloan Management Review* 50, no. 4 (2009): 62–69.

11. Siebdrat, Hoegl, and Ernst, "How to Manage Virtual Teams."

12. Lucy L. Gilson et al., "Virtual Teams Research: 10 Years, 10 Themes, and 10 Opportunities," *Journal of Management* 41, no. 5 (2015): 1313–1337, https://doi.org/10.1177/0149206314559946.

13. William H. A. Johnson et al., "Do Team Charters Help Team-Based Projects? The Effects of Team Charters on Performance and Satisfaction in Global Virtual Teams," *Academy of Management Learning & Education* 21, no. 2 (2022): 236–260, https://doi.org/10.5465/amle.2020.0332.

14. Stephen H. Courtright et al., "Quality Charters or Quality Members? A Control Theory Perspective on Team Charters and Team Performance," *Journal of Applied Psychology* 102, no. 10 (2017): 1462–1470, https://doi.org/10.1037/apl0000229.

15. Amy Edmondson, "Psychological Safety and Learning Behavior in Work Teams," *Administrative Science Quarterly* 44, no. 2 (1999): 350–383, https://doi.org/10.2307/2666999.

16. Bret H. Bradley et al., "Reaping the Benefits of Task Conflict in Teams: The Critical Role of Team Psychological Safety Climate," *Journal of Applied Psychology* 97, no. 1 (2012): 151–158, https://doi.org/10.1037/a0024200.

17. Charles Duhigg, "What Google Learned From Its Quest to Build the Perfect Team," *New York Times*, February 25, 2016, https://www.nytimes.com/2016/02/28/magazine/what-google-learned-from-its-quest-to-build-the-perfect-team.html.

18. Cristina B. Gibson and Jennifer L. Gibbs, "Unpacking the Concept of Virtuality: The Effects of Geographic Dispersion, Electronic Dependence, Dynamic Structure, and National

Diversity on Team Innovation," *Administrative Science Quarterly* 51, no. 3 (2006): 451–495, https://doi.org/10.2189/asqu.51.3.4.

19. Michael A. Roberto, "Lessons from Everest: The Interaction of Cognitive Bias, Psychological Safety, and System Complexity," *California Management Review* 45, no. 1 (2002): 136–158, https://doi.org/10.2307/41166157.

20. Catherine Durnell Cramton, "The Mutual Knowledge Problem and Its Consequences for Dispersed Collaboration," *Organization Science* 12, no. 3 (2001): 346–371, https://doi.org/10.1287/orsc.12.3.346.10098.

21. Manju K. Ahuja and John E. Galvin, "Socialization in Virtual Groups," *Journal of Management* 29, no. 2 (2003): 161–185, https://doi.org/10.1177/014920630302900203.

22. Christoph Riedl and A. Wooley, "Successful Remote Teams Communicate in Bursts," *Harvard Business Review*, October 28, 2020, https://hbr.org/2020/10/successful-remote-teams-communicate-in-bursts.

23. Laurel Farrer, "The Art of Asynchronous: Optimizing Efficiency In Remote Teams," *Forbes*, December 10, 2020, https://www.forbes.com/sites/laurelfarrer/2020/12/10/the-art-of-asynchronous-optimizing-efficiency-in-remote-teams/; Marcelo Lebre, "Why You Should Be Working Asynchronously in 2023," *Remote.com*, https://remote.com/blog/why-you-should-be-doing-async-work.

24. Richard L. Hughes, Robert C. Ginnett, and Gordon J. Curphy, "Contingency Theories of Leadership," in *Leading Organizations: Perspectives for a New Era*, ed. Gill Robinson Hickman (Thousand Oaks, CA: Sage Publications, 1998), 115–142.

25. Bradford S. Bell, Kristie L. McAlpine, and N. Sharon Hill, "Leading Virtually," *Annual Review of Organizational Psychology and Organizational Behavior* 10 (2023), https://doi.org/10.1146/annurev-orgpsych-120920-050115.

26. Radostina K. Purvanova et al., "Who Emerges into Virtual Team Leadership Roles? The Role of Achievement and Ascription Antecedents for Leadership Emergence across the

Virtuality Spectrum," *Journal of Business and Psychology* 36, no. 4 (2021): 713–733, https://doi.org/10.1007/s10869-020-09698-0.

27. Youngjin Yoo and Maryam Alavi, "Emergent Leadership in Virtual Teams: What Do Emergent Leaders Do?" *Information and Organization* 14, no. 1 (2004): 27–58, https://doi.org/10.1016/j.infoandorg.2003.11.001; Purvanova et al., "Who Emerges into Virtual Team Leadership Roles?"

28. Christina Breuer, Joachim Hüffmeier, and Guido Hertel, "Does Trust Matter More in Virtual Teams? A Meta-Analysis of Trust and Team Effectiveness Considering Virtuality and Documentation as Moderators," *Journal of Applied Psychology* 101, no. 8 (2016): 1151, https://doi.org/10.1037/apl0000113.

29. Timothy D. Golden and Sumita Raghuram, "Teleworker Knowledge Sharing and the Role of Altered Relational and Technological Interactions," *Journal of Organizational Behavior* 31, no. 8 (2010): 1061–1085, https://doi.org/10.1002/job.652.

30. Richard L. Daft, Robert H. Lengel, and Linda Klebe Trevino, "Message Equivocality, Media Selection, and Manager Performance: Implications for Information Systems," *MIS Quarterly* 11, no. 3 (1987): 355–366, https://doi.org/10.2307/248682.

31. The research of Joseph Walther perhaps best exemplifies these observations. One representative work is Walther, "Relational Aspects of Computer-Mediated Communication."

32. Debra Meyerson, Karl E. Weick, and Roderick M. Kramer, "Swift Trust and Temporary Groups," in *Trust in Organizations: Frontiers of Theory and Research*, ed. Roderick Kramer and Tom Tyler (Thousand Oaks, CA: Sage Publications, 1996), 166–195.

33. Sirkka L. Jarvenpaa and Dorothy E. Leidner, "Communication and Trust in Global Virtual Teams," *Organization Science* 10, no. 6 (1999): 791–815, https://doi.org/10.1287/orsc.10.6.791.

34. Jarvenpaa and Leidner, "Communication and Trust in Global Virtual Teams."

35. C. Brad Crisp and Sirkka L. Jarvenpaa, "Swift Trust in Global Virtual Teams: Trusting Beliefs and Normative Actions," *Journal of Personnel Psychology* 12, no. 1 (2013): 45–56, https://doi.org/10.1027/1866-5888/a000075.

36. Christina Breuer, Joachim Hüffmeier, and Guido Hertel, "Does Trust Matter More in Virtual Teams? A Meta-Analysis of Trust and Team Effectiveness Considering Virtuality and Documentation as Moderators," *Journal of Applied Psychology* 101, no. 8 (2016): 1151, https://doi.org/10.1037/apl0000113.

37. Gilson et al., "Virtual Teams Research."

38. Gibson and Gibbs, "Unpacking the Concept of Virtuality."

39. Ravi S. Gajendran and Aparna Joshi, "Innovation in Globally Distributed Teams: The Role of LMX, Communication Frequency, and Member Influence on Team Decisions," *Journal of Applied Psychology* 97, no. 6 (2012): 1252, https://doi.org/10.1037/a0028958.

40. Nicola Grözinger et al., "Innovation and Communication Media in Virtual Teams—An Experimental Study," *Journal of Economic Behavior & Organization* 180 (2020): 201–218, https://doi.org/10.2139/ssrn.3596685.

41. Brucks and Levav, "Virtual Communication Curbs Creative Idea Generation."

42. Sumita Raghuram et al., "Virtual Work: Bridging Research Clusters," *Academy of Management Annals* 13, no. 1 (2019): 308–341, https://doi.org/10.5465/annals.2017.0020.

43. Michael Boyer O'Leary and Mark Mortensen, "Go (Con) Figure: Subgroups, Imbalance, and Isolates in Geographically Dispersed Teams," *Organization Science* 21, no. 1 (2010): 115–131, https://doi.org/10.1287/orsc.1090.0434.

44. Nathan N. Bos et al., "In-Group/Out-Group Effects in Distributed Teams: An Experimental Simulation," *Proceedings of the 2004 ACM Conference on Computer Supported Cooperative Work* (2004): 429–436, https://doi.org/10.1145/1031607.1031679.

45. Jeffrey T. Polzer et al., "Extending the Faultline Model to Geographically Dispersed Teams: How Co-located Subgroups

Can Impair Group Functioning," *Academy of Management Journal* 49, no. 4 (2006): 679–692, https://doi.org/10.5465/AMJ.2006.22083024.

Chapter 6

1. Timothy Golden and John Veiga, "The Impact of Extent of Telecommuting on Job Satisfaction: Resolving Inconsistent Findings," *Journal of Management* 31, no. 2 (2005): 301–318, https://doi.org/10.1177/0149206304271768.

2. Sara Korolevich, *The State of Remote Work in 2021: A Survey of the American Workforce* (Redwood City, CA: Goodhire, 2021), https://www.goodhire.com/resources/articles/state-of-remote-work-survey/; Ernst & Young, "More Than Half of Employees Globally Would Quit Their Jobs If Not Provided Post-pandemic Flexibility, EY Survey Finds," press release, May 12, 2021, https://www.ey.com/en_gl/news/2021/05/more-than-half-of-employees-globally-would-quit-their-jobs-if-not-provided-post-pandemic-flexibility-ey-survey-finds.

3. Jose Maria Barrero et al., *The Shift to Remote Work Lessens Wage-Growth Pressures*, No. w30197, National Bureau of Economic Research, 2022.

4. Roy Maurer, "Viewpoint: Hot Desking Is Not Genuine Flexible-Work Model," *SHRM*, March 28, 2022, https://www.shrm.org/hr-today/news/hr-news/pages/hot-desking-is-not-genuine-flexible-work-model.aspx.

5. Jena McGregor, "Five Trends That Are Shaping What Your Office Looks Like," *Washington Post*, June 15, 2015, https://www.washingtonpost.com/news/on-leadership/wp/2015/06/15/five-trends-that-are-reshaping-what-your-office-looks-like/.

6. Bob Fox, "CEOs Talk Workplace: Interview with Kevin Virostek of EY," *Work Design Magazine*, March 1, 2018, https://www.workdesign.com/2018/03/ceo-talk-workplace-kevin-virostek-ey/.

7. Nicole Lewis, "Hot Desking and Hoteling Software Is in Demand," *SHRM*, October 18, 2021, https://www.shrm.org/

resourcesandtools/hr-topics/technology/pages/hot-desk
ing-hoteling-software-is-in-demand.aspx.

8. Natalie Healey, "Hot Desking Was Meant to Save Us
All Time and Money. It Hasn't," *Wired*, February 17, 2020,
https://www.wired.co.uk/article/hot-desking-meaning-
benefits.

9. This section focuses on concerns about the impact on a
company's business. Many company leaders also have
concerns about remote work's potentially negative effects on
individual employee well-being, such as feelings of isolation
and increased work–life conflict. These concerns have been
covered in considerable detail already in Chapters 3 and 4 of
this text.

10. Jack Kelly, "Instead of Quitting, Workers Are Ghosting
Coasting, Slacking and Cyberloafing," *Forbes*, April 1, 2022,
https://www.forbes.com/sites/jackkelly/2022/04/01/work
ers-are-ghost-coasting-slacking-and-cyberloafing-instead-of-
quitting/.

11. Samantha Delouya, "From 'Quiet Quitting' to 'Career
Cushioning,' Here Are the Workplace Trends That Took 2022
by Storm—and Whether They'll Continue in 2023," *Business
Insider*, December 20, 2022, https://www.businessinsider.
com/workplace-trends-2022-quiet-quitting-career-cushion
ing-great-resignation-labor-2022-12.

12. Microsoft, *Hybrid Work Is Just Work. Are We Doing It Wrong?*
(Redmond, WA: Microsoft, 2022), 4–5.

13. Bloom et al., "Does Working from Home Work?"; Choudhury,
Foroughi, and Larson, "Work-from-Anywhere."

14. Sirkka Jarvenpaa and Dorothy Leidner, "Communication
and Trust in Global Virtual Teams," *Organization Science* 10,
no. 6 (1999): 791–815, https://doi.org/10.1287/orsc.10.6.791;
Kannan Srikanth and Phanish Puranam, "Integrating
Distributed Work: Comparing Task Design, Communication,
and Tacit Coordination Mechanisms," *Strategic Management
Journal* 32, no. 8 (2011): 849–875, https://doi.org/10.1002/
smj.908.

15. Katie Johnson, "The Remote Work Conundrum: Employees Want It, but Is It Good for Them," *Boston Globe*, February 22, 2023, https://www.bostonglobe.com/2023/02/22/busin ess/remote-work-conundrum-employees-want-it-is-it-good-them/.

16. Barrero et al., *The Shift to Remote Work*.

17. Sarah Forbes et al., *Flexible Working and the Future of Work: Managing Employees since COVID-19* (Birmingham, UK: Equal Parenting Project, 2022).

18. Barrero et al., *Shift to Remote Work*.

19. Autonomy is a significant motivator for most people; therefore, an increase in autonomy generally increases motivation and a decrease in autonomy generally decreases motivation. (Hackman and Oldham 1980).

20. Amy Hackney et al., "Working in the Digital Economy: A Systematic Review of the Impact of Work from Home Arrangements on Personal and Organizational Performance and Productivity," *PLOS One* 17, no. 10 (October 2022): https://doi.org/10.1371/journal.pone.0274728.

21. Chee-Wee Koh, Tammy D. Allen, and Nina Zafar, "Dissecting Reasons for Not Telecommuting: Are Nonusers a Homogenous Group?" *The Psychologist-Manager Journal* 16, no. 4 (2013): 243, https://doi.org/10.1037/mgr0000008.

22. Koh, Allen, and Zafar, "Dissecting Reasons."

23. Matthew Boyle, "Rebranding RTO: Why Companies Coin Names for Their Hybrid-Work Plans," *Bloomberg*, January 17, 2023, https://www.bloomberg.com/news/articles/2023-01-17/hybrid-work-plan-names-show-corporate-conc ern-about-flex-work.

24. Laurel Farrer, "Is Remote Work Illegal?" *Forbes*, April 30, 2019, https://www.forbes.com/sites/laurelfarrer/2019/04/30/is-remote-work-illegal/?sh=6906b27d4442.

25. Alex Christian, "The Simmering Tension between Remote and In-office Workers," *BBC*, April 11, 2022, https://www.bbc.com/worklife/article/20220408-the-simmering-tension-between-remote-and-in-office-workers.

26. Samantha Delouya and Avery Hartmans, "Resentment Is Mounting as Some Employees Are Forced Back to the Office and Some Are Allowed to Work from Home," *MSN*, November 1, 2022, https://www.msn.com/en-us/lifestyle/career/resentment-is-mounting-as-some-employees-are-forced-back-to-the-office-and-some-are-allowed-to-work-from-home/ar-AA13BIQx?li=BBnbcA0.

27. Julianna Pillemer and Nancy P. Rothbard, "Friends without Benefits: Understanding the Dark Sides of Workplace Friendship," *Academy of Management Review* 43, no. 4 (2018): 635–660, https://doi.org/10.5465/amr.2016.0309.

28. Michael Kolomatsky, "Remote Work Opens Up Cheaper Housing Options," *New York Times*, February 10, 2022, https://www.nytimes.com/2022/02/10/realestate/remote-work-housing.html.

29. Kate Conger, "Facebook Starts Planning for Permanent Remote Workers," *New York Times*, May 21, 2020, https://www.nytimes.com/2020/05/21/technology/facebook-remote-work-coronavirus.html.

30. Alex Christian, "Companies Are Grappling over Whether Fully Remote Employees Should Be Paid the Same as In-Office Staff. What Is the Right Way Forward?" *BBC*, January 31, 2022, https://www.bbc.com/worklife/article/20220127-location-based-salary.

31. Christian, "Companies Are Grappling."

32. Stephen Miller, "Remote Workers Expect Pay to Reflect Their Locations," *SHRM*, April 21, 2021, https://www.shrm.org/ResourcesAndTools/hr-topics/compensation/Pages/remote-workers-expect-pay-to-reflect-their-locations.aspx.

33. Foundry, *Future of Work Study 2022* (New York: Foundry, 2022), https://resources.foundryco.com/download/future-of-work-executive-summary.

34. Gartner, "Gartner Forecasts Worldwide IT Spending to Grow 3% in 2022," press release, July 14, 2022, https://www.gartner.com/en/newsroom/press-releases/2022-06-14-gartner-forecasts-worldwide-it-spending-to-grow-3-percent-in-2022.

35. Jill Duffy, "The Best Online Collaboration Software for 2023," *PC Magazine*, January 11, 2023, https://www.pcmag.com/picks/the-best-online-collaboration-software.

36. Linda Rosencrance, "How to Choose the Right Project Collaboration Software," *Computerworld*, January 26, 2022, https://www.computerworld.com/article/3647528/how-to-choose-the-right-project-collaboration-software.html.

37. Lewis, "Hot Desking."

38. Laurence Goasduff, "Hybrid and Remote Workers Change How They Use IT Equipment," *Gartner*, July 13, 2021, https://www.gartner.com/smarterwithgartner/hybrid-and-remote-workers-change-how-they-use-it-equipment.

39. Chris DeRamus, "The Cloud Is the Backbone of Remote Work," *Forbes*, June 16, 2020, https://www.forbes.com/sites/forbestechcouncil/2020/06/16/the-cloud-is-the-backbone-of-remote-work.

40. Tatum Hunter, "Here Are All the Ways Your Boss Can Legally Monitor You," *Washington Post*, August 20, 2021, https://www.washingtonpost.com/technology/2021/08/20/work-from-home-computer-monitoring/.

41. Simon Migliano, "Employee Surveillance Software Demand Up 55% since Pandemic Started," *Top10VPN.com*, February 13, 2023, https://www.top10vpn.com/research/covid-employee-surveillance/.

42. Rudolf Siegel, Cornelius J. König, and Veronika Lazar, "The Impact of Electronic Monitoring on Employees' Job Satisfaction, Stress, Performance, and Counterproductive Work Behavior: A Meta-Analysis," *Computers in Human Behavior Reports* 8 (2022): 100227, https://doi.org/10.1016/j.chbr.2022.100227.

43. Jeffrey M. Stanton, "Reactions to Employee Performance Monitoring: Framework, Review, and Research Directions," *Human Performance* 13, no. 1 (2000): 85–113, https://doi.org/10.1207/S15327043HUP1301_4.

44. Stanton, "Reactions."

45. Daniel M. Ravid et al., "EPM 20/20: A Review, Framework, and Research Agenda for Electronic Performance Monitoring," *Journal of Management* 46, no. 1 (2020): 100–126, https://doi.org/10.1177/0149206319869435.

46. Ravid et al., "EPM 20/20."

47. Chase E. Thiel et al., "Stripped of Agency: The Paradoxical Effect of Employee Monitoring on Deviance," *Journal of Management* 49, no. 2 (2023): 709–740, https://doi.org/10.1177/01492063211053224.

48. "RadioShack Layoff Notices Are Sent by E-Mail," *New York Times*, August 31, 2006, https://www.nytimes.com/2006/08/31/business/31radio.html.

49. Tristan Bove, "Former Google Worker Recorded a Before-and-After of Her Layoff in Dueling TikTok Videos That Went from Free Food and Tiki Bars to Locked Email and Tears," *Fortune*, January 23, 2023, https://fortune.com/2023/01/23/google-layoffs-ex-employee-records-video-tiktok-experience-before-and-after-perks/.

50. Matt Day and Spencer Soper, "Amazon Kicks Off Round of Job Cuts Affecting 18,000 People," *Los Angeles Times*, January 18, 2023, https://www.latimes.com/business/story/2023-01-18/amazon-job-cuts-18000-people; Jena McGregor, "Forget Zoom Layoffs. Job Cuts by Email Are Tech's Latest Digital Pink Slip," *Forbes*, February 1, 2023, https://www.forbes.com/sites/jenamcgregor/2023/02/01/forget-zoom-layoffs-job-cuts-by-email-are-techs-latest-digital-pink-slip/.

51. McGregor, "Forget Zoom Layoffs."

52. Daniel Skarlicki and Robert Folger, "Retaliation in the Workplace: The Roles of Distributive, Procedural, and Interactional Justice," *Journal of Applied Psychology* 82, no. 3 (1997): 434, https://doi.org/10.1037/0021-9010.82.3.434.

Chapter 7

1. Nilles, "Telecommunications and Organizational Decentralization"; Nilles, *The Telecommunications–Transportation Tradeoff*.

2. Tsugio Makimoto and David Manners, *Digital Nomad* (Hoboken, NJ: Wiley, 1997).

3. Prithwiraj Choudhury, Emma Salomon, and Brittany Logan, "Tulsa Remote: Moving Talent to Middle America," Harvard Business School Case 621–048, September 2020 (revised July 2022), https://www.hbs.edu/faculty/Pages/item.aspx?num=58687.

4. Personal correspondence, February 14, 2023.

5. "Federal Agencies Return to Office by Leveraging Telework," *Thomson Reuters*, August 5, 2022, https://legal.thomsonreut ers.com/blog/federal-agencies-return-to-office-by-leverag ing-telework/; Ainslie Cruickshank, "COVID Pandemic-19 Shows Telecommuting Can Help Fight Climate Change," *Scientific American*, July 22, 2022, https://www.scientificameri can.com/article/covid-19-pandemic-shows-telecommuting-can-help-fight-climate-change/.

6. P. Bhanumati, Mark de Haan, and James William Tebrake, "Greenhouse Emissions Rise to Record, Erasing Drop during Pandemic," *IMFBlog*, June 30, 2022, https://www.imf.org/en/Blogs/Articles/2022/06/30/greenhouse-emissions-rise-to-record-erasing-drop-during-pandemic.

7. Data from the US Energy Information Administration's consumption and efficiency material statistics, accessed February 2, 2023, available at https://www.eia.gov/cons umption/.

8. Andrew Hook et al., "A Systematic Review of the Energy and Climate Impacts of Teleworking," *Environmental Research Letters* 15, no. 9 (2020), https://doi.org/10.1088/1748-9326/ab8a84.

9. S. Whitaker, "Did the COVID-19 Pandemic Cause an Urban Exodus?" District Data Brief, Federal Reserve Bank of Cleveland, February 5, 2021. https://www.clevelandfed.org/publications/cleveland-fed-district-data-brief/cfddb-20210 205-did-the-covid-19-pandemic-cause-an-urban-exodus.

10. Benjamin Goldstein, Dimitrios Gounaridis, and Joshua P. Newell, "The Carbon Footprint of Household Energy Use

in the United States," *Proceedings of the National Academy of Sciences* 117, no. 32 (2020): 19122–19130, https://doi.org/10.1073/pnas.1922205117. A less common, and more extreme, version of this are work-from-anywhere employees who migrate to different parts of the country but still regularly travel (often via environmentally challenging airplanes) to their home offices.

11. Hook et al., "A Systematic Review of the Energy and Climate."

12. "Office vs Home Working: How We Can Save Our Carbon Footprint," *WSP*, February 20, 2020, https://www.wsp.com/en-gb/insights/office-vs-home-working-how-we-can-save-our-carbon-footprint.

13. "Most Used Heating Methods in the United Kingdom, 2022," *Statista Research*, January 31, 2023, https://www.statista.com/statistics/426988/united-kingdom-uk-heating-methods/.

14. The authors of this analysis did not attempt to generalize their findings beyond the United Kingdom. What more typically occurs is an outside party taking findings from a localized study such as this, and inaccurately generalizing them to a larger, or very different population.

15. "Nearly 90% of U.S. Households Used Air Conditioning in 2020," US Energy Information Administration, May 31, 2022, https://www.eia.gov/todayinenergy/detail.php?id=52558.

16. Alba Badia et al., "A Take-home Message from COVID-19 on Urban Air Pollution Reduction through Mobility Limitations and Teleworking," *NPJ Urban Sustainability* 1, no. 35 (2021), https://doi.org/10.1038/s42949-021-00037-7.

17. Gianni De Fraja et al., "Remote Working and the New Geography of Local Service Spending," CEPR Discussion Paper DP17431, July 3, 2022, https://cepr.org/publications/dp17431.

18. Mark Johnson, "The Small Cities and Towns Booming from Remote Work," *BBC*, January 26, 2022, https://www.bbc.com/worklife/article/20220125-the-small-cities-and-towns-booming-from-remote-work.

19. Emily Peck, "Remote Workers Pushed Up Incomes and Home Prices in These Cities," *Axios*, August 4, 2022, https://www.axios.com/2022/08/04/remote-workers-pushed-up-incomes-and-home-prices-in-these-cities; Patrick Sisson, "Remote Workers Spur an Affordable Housing Crunch in Montana," *Bloomberg News*, February 2, 2021, https://www.bloomberg.com/news/articles/2021-02-11/the-zoom-town-boom-in-bozeman-montana.

20. Alberto Fajardo, Roberto Ramirez, and Josue Gonzalez, "Boon or Threat? Mexico City Wrestles with Influx of Remote U.S. Workers," *Reuters*, September 13, 2022, https://www.reuters.com/world/americas/boon-or-threat-mexico-city-wrestles-with-influx-remote-us-workers-2022-09-13/.

21. Johnson, "The Small Cities and Towns Booming from Remote Work."

22. Lin Grensing-Pophal, "Taking Advantage of a Broader Talent Pool," SHRM, February 3, 2021, https://www.shrm.org/resourcesandtools/hr-topics/talent-acquisition/pages/taking-advantage-of-a-broader-talent-pool.aspx.

23. Diederik Baazil and Pablo Fernandez Cras, "Dutch House Approves to Make Work from Home a Legal Right," *Bloomberg News*, July 5, 2022, https://www.bloomberg.com/news/articles/2022-07-05/dutch-parliament-approves-to-make-work-from-home-a-legal-right.

24. "Netherlands Poised to Make Work-from-Home a Legal Right," *Wall Street Journal*, July 7, 2022, https://www.wsj.com/articles/netherlands-poised-to-make-work-from-home-a-legal-right-11657206737.

25. Lucy Papachristou, "New Remote Working Legislation around the World," *Global Compliance News*, January 24, 2023, https://globalnews.lockton.com/new-remote-working-legislation-around-the-world/.

26. Sofia Bargellini and Claudia Di Biase, "Legal Update: Remote Work in Italy: Where Are We Now?" Seyfarth Shaw LLP, August 3, 2022, https://www.seyfarth.com/news-insights/legal-update-remote-work-in-italy-where-are-we-now.html.

27. Jack Kelly, "Belgium, Portugal and Other European Countries Prohibit Managers from Contacting Employees Outside of Working Hours," *Forbes*, February 2, 2022, https://www.for bes.com/sites/jackkelly/2022/02/03/belgium-portugal-and-other-european-countries-are-ahead-of-the-us-prohibit ing-managers-from-contacting-employees-outside-of-work ing-hours/?sh=2a81d89b1d00.

28. "Implications of 'Work from Anywhere'—When Remote Workers Cross State Lines," *ADP*, June 2022, https://www.adp.com/spark/articles/2022/06/implications-of-work-from-anywhere-when-remote-workers-cross-state-lines.aspx#.

29. Jesse G. Pauker, "Mandatory Remote Working—Can Employers Force Their Employees to Work from Their Homes?" Client alert, King & Spaulding, November 30, 2022, https://www.kslaw.com/news-and-insights/mandat ory-remote-working-can-employers-force-their-employ ees-to-work-from-their-homes.

30. Pauker, "Mandatory Remote Working."

31. Jeanne Sahadi, "Working Remotely in a Different State than Your Employer? Here's What That Means for Your Taxes," *CNN Business*, March 1, 2022, https://www.cnn.com/2022/03/01/success/state-income-tax-ramifications-remote-work/index.html.

32. Scott Lincicome and Ilana Blumsack, *Remote Work* (Washington, DC: Cato Institute, December 2022), https://www.cato.org/publications/remote-work.

33. Tracey Johnson, "49 Countries With Digital Nomad Visas—The Ultimate List," *Nomad Girl*, November 25, 2022, https://nomadgirl.co/countries-with-digital-nomad-visas/.

34. Hannah Towey, "From Portugal to Bali, These 28 Countries and Territories Offer 'Digital Nomad Visas' for Remote Workers," *Business Insider*, December 8, 2022, https://www.businessinsider.com/countries-with-digital-nomad-visas-list-income-requirements-spain-portugal-malta-12.

35. R. de la Feria and G. Maffini, "The Impact of Digitalisation on Personal Income Taxes," *British Tax Review* 2 (April 2021): 154–168, https://doi.org/10.2139/ssrn.3835095.

36. "Cross-border Hybrid and Remote Working—What's Next?" *KPMG*, November 14, 2022, https://home.kpmg/uk/en/home/insights/2022/11/tmd-cross-border-hybrid-and-remote-working-what-next.html.

37. Organisation for Economic Co-operation and Development, "Tax Administration: Towards Sustainable Remote Working in a Post COVID-19 Environment," July 19, 2021, https://www.oecd.org/coronavirus/policy-responses/tax-administration-towards-sustainable-remote-working-in-a-post-covid-19-environment-fdc0844d/.

38. Daniel McCue, "The Possible Impacts of Remote Work on Cities, Neighborhoods, and Households," Harvard Joint Center for Housing Studies, November 8, 2021, https://www.jchs.harvard.edu/blog/possible-impacts-remote-work-cities-neighborhoods-and-households.

39. Tim Henderson, "As Remote Work Persists, Cities Struggle to Adapt," *Stateline*, May 24, 2022, https://www.pewtrusts.org/en/research-and-analysis/blogs/stateline/2022/05/24/as-remote-work-persists-cities-struggle-to-adapt.

40. Anna Johnson, "ND Attracting Remote workers," *KFYRTV*, December 13, 2021, https://www.kfyrtv.com/2021/12/13/nd-attracting-remote-workers/.

41. "Telecommuter Forward! Certification," Minnesota Department of Employment and Economic Development, https://mn.gov/deed/programs-services/broadband/telecommuter-forward/.

42. Choudhury, Salomon, and Logan, "Tulsa Remote."

43. "Lessons from a Leading Remote Work Incentive in Tulsa, Oklahoma," Economic Innovation Group, https://eig.org/tulsa-remote/.

44. Prithwiraj Choudhury, Evan Starr, and Thomaz Teodorovicz, "Work-from-Anywhere as a Public Policy: 3 Findings from

the Tulsa Remote Program," Brookings Institution, September 15, 2022, https://www.brookings.edu/research/work-from-anywhere-as-a-public-policy-three-findings-from-the-tulsa-remote-program/.

45. Jon Kamp, "Remote Workers Can Live Anywhere. These Cities (and Small Towns) Are Luring Them with Perks," *Wall Street Journal*, October 9, 2021, https://www.wsj.com/articles/remote-workers-can-live-anywhere-these-cities-and-small-towns-are-luring-them-with-perks-11633820638. Austyn Gaffney, "Incentive Programs Have Lured Thousands of Remote Workers from Major Metro Areas to Small Cities," *Smart Cities Dive*, August 1, 2022, https://www.smartcitiesd ive.com/news/cities-worker-incentive-relocation-programs-tulsa-remote-choose-topeka/628537/.

46. "These Countries Are Paying People to Move to the Countryside," World Economic Forum, April 13, 2022, https://www.weforum.org/agenda/2022/04/countries-pay ing-you-to-move-to-countryside/.

47. Walter Frick, "Tulsa's Big Bet on Remote Workers," *Harvard Business Review*, January 13, 2023, https://hbr.org/2023/01/tulsas-big-bet-on-remote-workers.

Chapter 8

1. Jose Maria Barrero et al., *Benchmarking SWAA Estimates of the Prevalence of Working from Home* (WFH Research, 2023), 2, https://wfhresearch.com/wp-content/uploads/2023/01/Benchmarking_SWAA.pdf.

2. Sarah Kessler, "Getting Rid of Remote Work Will Take More than a Downturn," *New York Times*, January 7, 2023, https://www.nytimes.com/2023/01/07/business/dealbook/remote-work-downturn.html.

3. Barrero, Bloom, and Davis, "Why Working from Home Will Stick."

4. Armani Syed, "These Companies Have Announced the Biggest Layoffs in 2023," *Time*, January 20, 2023, https://time.com/6248866/google-alphabet-biggest-layoffs-2023/.

5. Jose Maria Barrero et al., "The Shift to Remote Work Lessens Wage-Growth Pressures," NBER Working Paper No. 30197, 2022, https://doi/10.3386/w30197.

6. Sarah Perez, "Walmart Introduces Virtual Try-on Tech Which Uses Customers' Own Photos to Model the Clothing," *Tech Crunch*, September 15, 2022, https://techcrunch.com/2022/09/14/walmart-introduces-virtual-try-on-tech-which-uses-customers-own-photos-to-model-the-clothing/.

7. Katie Holdefehr, "These Innovative Apps Help You Visualize Furniture in Your Home before You Buy It," *Real Simple*, June 29, 2022, https://www.realsimple.com/home-organizing/decorating/augmented-reality-furniture-shopping-apps.

8. *For US Manufacturing, Virtual Reality Is for Real* (New York: Price Waterhouse Coopers, 2016), 2, https://www.pwc.com/us/en/industrial-products/publications/assets/augmented-virtual-reality-next-manufacturing-pwc.pdf.

9. Other metaverse applications, in particular gaming and entertainment, remain focused on headset-based applications, given their superior sensory richness.

10. Personal interview with Leslie Shannon, January 23, 2023.

11. Monica Soliman, Johanna Peetz, and Mariya Davydenko, "The Impact of Immersive Technology on Nature Relatedness and Pro-Environmental Behavior," *Journal of Media Psychology* 29, no. 1 (2017): 8–17, https://doi.org/10.1027/1864-1105/a000213; Ayoung Suh and Jane Prophet, "The State of Immersive Technology Research: A Literature Analysis," *Computers in Human Behavior* 86 (2018): 77–90, https://doi.org/10.1016/j.chb.2018.04.019; Hyuck-Gi Lee, Sungwon Chung, and Won-Hee Lee, "Presence in Virtual Golf Simulators: The Effects of Presence on Perceived Enjoyment, Perceived Value, and Behavioral Intention," *New Media & Society* 15, no. 6 (2013): 930–946, https://doi.org/10.1177/1461444812464033.

12. Shannon interview.

13. Megan Leonhardt, "Accenture Designed Its Own Metaverse for Employees, Complete with Exact Replicas of Offices,"

Fortune, April 11, 2022, https://fortune.com/2022/04/11/accenture-builds-corporate-metaverse/.

14. Katie Johnson, "Who Needs an Office? Companies Ditch Headquarters and Connect Workers Remotely," *Boston Globe*, October 3, 2019, https://www.bostonglobe.com/business/2019/10/03/who-needs-office-companies-ditch-headquarters-and-connect-workers-remotely/JJxcjwyveEzGtUeajqqfTN/story.html.

15. "South Korea: Metaverse Offices Are the Future of Work, According to Zigbang Execs," *Japan News*, July 21, 2022, https://japannews.yomiuri.co.jp/world/asia-pacific/20220721-51702/.

16. Prithwiraj Choudhury and Susie L. Ma, *Unilever: Remote Work in Manufacturing* (Cambridge, MA: Harvard Business Press), https://www.hbsp.harvard.edu/product/622030-PDF-ENG?Ntt=.

17. Annie Brown, "The Future Of AI-Driven Meeting Technology," *Forbes*, October 4, 2021, https://www.forbes.com/sites/anniebrown/2021/10/04/the-future-of-ai-driven-meeting-technology/?sh=eb92b0e287a2; Keith Lang, "10 Ways AI Assistants Can Help with Your Meetings & Interviews," *Fat Frog Media*, December 21, 2022, https://fatfrogmedia.com/ai-meeting-assistants/.

18. "FAQs," Headroom. https://www.goheadroom.com/faqs.

19. *Digital Nomads* (Bee Cave, TX: MBO Partners, 2022), https://www.mbopartners.com/state-of-independence/digital-nomads/. MBO Partners, which runs a job platform for independent contractors, estimated that some 16.9 million people originating from the United States worked as digital nomads in 2022. The survey of digital nomads is the most complete of its type; however, the survey extrapolates results based on a much smaller number of digital nomads only residing in the United States at the time of the survey. The extrapolated numbers may be inflated, and readers should interpret these results with care. However, the true number of digital nomads is likely at least in the millions. Another

survey, conducted by the website A Brother Abroad in 2023, estimated that there were thirty-five million digital nomads worldwide, of which 10.8 million originated in the United States.

20. Jessica Elliott, "What Is a Digital Nomad?" U.S. Chamber of Commerce, 2023, https://www.uschamber.com/co/grow/thrive/what-is-a-digital-nomad#.

21. Rachael Woldoff and Robert Litchfield, *Digital Nomads: In Search of Freedom, Community, and Meaningful Work in the New Economy* (New York: Oxford University Press, 2021).

22. Jonathan Beckman, "Don't Settle: The Rise of Digital Nomads," *The Economist*, March 21, 2018, https://www.economist.com/1843/2018/03/21/dont-settle-the-rise-of-digital-nomads.

23. Prithwiraj (Raj) Choudhury, "How 'Digital Nomad' Visas Can Boost Local Economies," *Harvard Business Review*, May 27, 2022, https://hbr.org/2022/05/how-digital-nomad-visas-can-boost-local-economies.

24. Daryl Hirsch and Mindi Hirsch, "Why We Loved and Quit the Digital Nomad Life," *2foodtrippers.com*, https://www.2foodtrippers.com/digital-nomad-life/; "Digital Nomad Interview: Dr. Willy Portier, Online Entrepreneur," *Bright Nomad*, November 5, 2022, https://brightnomad.net/digital-nomad-entrepreneur-interview-willy-portier/; Woldoff and Litchfield, *Digital Nomads*.

25. Mary Lou Costa, "The Rise of Digital Nomad Families," *BBC*, June 16, 2022, https://www.bbc.com/worklife/article/20220615-the-rise-of-digital-nomad-families.

26. Christopher Elliott, "What I Wish I Had Known before I Started Traveling with Teenagers," *Washington Post*, May 12, 2022, https://www.washingtonpost.com/travel/2022/05/12/travel-vacation-teens-family/.

27. Rachel Feintzeig, "People Who Work from Home Have a Secret: They Have Two Jobs," *Wall Street Journal*, August 13, 2021, https://www.wsj.com/articles/these-peo

ple-who-work-from-home-have-a-secret-they-have-two-jobs-11628866529.

28. Robin Madell, "Should You Work 2 Remote Jobs at Once?" *U.S. News & World Report*, December 30, 2022, https://money.usnews.com/money/blogs/outside-voices-careers/articles/should-you-work-multiple-remote-jobs-at-once.

29. Feintzeig, "People Who Work from Home Have a Secret."

30. Alexandre Tanzi, "Over 5 Million New US Startups Show Covid-Era Boom Has Legs," *Bloomberg*, January 17, 2023, https://www.bloomberg.com/news/articles/2023-01-17/over-5-million-new-us-startups-show-covid-era-boom-has-legs.

31. Rani Molla, "The Rise of the Side Startup," *Vox*, August 11, 2022, https://www.vox.com/recode/23299590/side-startup-remote-workers-founding-businesses-while-employed.

32. *2021 Integrated Annual Report* (Brooklyn, NY: Etsy Inc., 2021), 10.

33. Johnson, "Who Needs an Office?"

34. "Why GitLab Uses the Term All-remote to Describe Its 100% Remote Workforce," GitLab, https://about.gitlab.com/company/culture/all-remote/terminology/.

35. "7 in 10 Businesses Have Permanently Closed Office Space during the Pandemic," *Digital.com*, https://digital.com/businesses-permanently-closing-office-space-during-the-pandemic/.

INDEX

For the benefit of digital users, indexed terms that span two pages (e.g., 52–53) may, on occasion, appear on only one of those pages.